Caring for Sexually Abused Children

A HANDBOOK FOR FAMILIES & CHURCHES

DR. R. TIMOTHY KEARNEY

IVP Books

An imprint of InterVarsity Press
Downers Grove, Illinois

InterVarsity Press
P.O. Box 1400, Downers Grove, IL 60515-1426
World Wide Web: www.ivpress.com
E-mail: email@ivpress.com

InterVarsity Press® *is the book-publishing division of InterVarsity Christian Fellowship/USA*®*, a movement of students and faculty active on campus at hundreds of universities, colleges and schools of nursing in the United States of America, and a member movement of the International Fellowship of Evangelical Students. For information about local and regional activities, write Public Relations Dept., InterVarsity Christian Fellowship/USA, 6400 Schroeder Rd., P.O. Box 7895, Madison, WI 53707-7895, or visit the IVCF website at <www.intervarsity.org>.*

All Scripture quotations, unless otherwise indicated, are taken from the Holy Bible, New International Version®*.* NIV®*. Copyright* ©*1973, 1978, 1984 by International Bible Society. Used by permission of Zondervan Publishing House. All rights reserved.*

Cover photograph: Nina Shannon/iStockphoto

ISBN 978-0-8308-2246-1

Printed in the United States of America ∞

InterVarsity Press is committed to protecting the environment and to the responsible use of natural resources. As a member of the Green Press Initiative we use recycled paper whenever possible. To learn more about the Green Press Initiative, visit <www.greenpressinitiative .org>.

Library of Congress Cataloging-in-Publication Data

Kearney, R. Timothy, 1954-
    Caring for sexually abused children: a handbook for families & churches/R. Timothy Kearney.
        p. cm.
    ISBN 0-8308-2246-1 (alk. paper)
        1. Sexually abused children—Rehabilitation—Handbooks, manuals, etc.   2. Sexually abused children—Services for—Handbooks, manuals, etc. 3. Child sexual abuse—Prevention—Handbooks, manuals, etc. 4. Christian life. I. Title.
    RJ507.S49 K42 2001
    618.92'85836—dc21

                                                                                    00-06734

P	22	21	20	19	18	17	16	15	14	13	12	11	10	9	8	7
Y	24	23	22	21	20	19	18	17	16	15	14	13	12	11	10	

To Jennifer.
Without your love, faith and encouragement
this would not be.

CONTENTS

Acknowledgments

I am tempted to name here everyone who helped to form who I am today, and who thus, directly or indirectly, was a part of the shaping of this book. God has richly blessed me with friends and colleagues for whom I am truly grateful. While there is not time or space to list you all, I would particularly like to thank:

The clients with whom I have had the privilege of working during the past twenty years. We have stood on holy ground together, working toward healing and restoration in the midst of much pain. For reasons of confidentiality I cannot mention names, but please know that your lives have taught and inspired me.

Charlie and Anne Hummel. Thank you for encouraging me to write the book I've carried in my head for years, and for your many helpful criticisms and suggestions.

InterVarsity Press—especially Jim Hoover for taking the book on and Linda Doll for shaping and forming the manuscript into a finished project with such grace and dexterity that it has left me astonished that editors are ever viewed negatively.

My colleagues Tom Ruotolo, Barbara Burgess, Amal Tanahgo, Jude Benedict and Jane Nichols at Shoreline Christian Counseling, and the pastors and board of the Southern Connecticut Christian Network, for their support and prayer.

*   *   *

Many friends who brainstormed problems and solutions, and who prayed for me and my family throughout the writing of this book, especially:

Linda and Mark MacGougan for walking with me on the long road from the conception of the idea to the final product, for reading and commenting on the manuscript, and for never being more than a phone call away when help was needed.

Alinda and Bevan Stanley for their faithfulness in prayer and their love for my whole family.

Judy and Scott Grillo for their encouragement (and help in buying a car when I had no time to leave the word processor to look for one).

Hua-Chin and Dick Kantzer for being there to listen and to pray.

Sue and Bob Britton for their prayers and constancy as they have remained a part of my life and work telephonically.

Linda Hanick for her common sense, concrete advice and resourcefulness.

It is a tremendous blessing to have such friends.

Intercessors at Breakthrough Intercessors who helped to pray this into being.

*   *   *

Most especially my family:

My daughters, Elizabeth and Anne, who have relinquished time with me so that I could write, and who fill my life with joy and laughter.

And my wife, Jennifer, who is God's greatest gift to me in this life. She has been constant in her support and prayers for me-talking through ideas and tough spots, giving advice and editorial assistance, keeping our home running smoothly, and picking up the slack so that I could step aside from family time to write.

I am grateful to all of these people and appreciate all they have done to support me and to further the completion of this book. It is my hope and prayer that it will be of help to those walking through the trauma of sexual abuse in their family and those working with sexually abused children and their families.

Introduction

When Child Sexual Abuse Intrudes

Laura is a twenty-eight-year-old mother of two young children. Suzie is five, and Tommy just turned three. After Andy rushed out to work, she put the kids in for a quick bath so that they would both be clean in time for her to go to the Bible study at First Church. While washing her daughter's hair, Suzie looked up and asked her if she would wash her "pee-pee" too. Being rushed for time, Laura told her daughter that she was old enough to wash herself there and asked her to do it so they could get out the door on time. But Suzie persisted and told her mother that she liked it when the sitter washed her there—it felt good.

What's a parent to do in a situation like this? Laura's first thought was to wonder why the sitter was even giving Suzie and Tommy baths. Then it hit her that her daughter might have been molested. What question should she ask to find out? Should she even be the one to ask questions? What would help or hurt her daughter most? Could Tommy be being touched too, or was he too young? She trusted the sitter, but shouldn't she believe her daughter? She knew so little about sexual abuse beyond the numbers that were out in the media. And who could she turn to for support with all this? Was her husband, Andy, her God-given support—or should she suspect even him? Why had God let something happen to her children—if anything had—when she tried so hard to live her life as she should? All these—and a hundred more questions—ran through her head as she raced for the phone to call Andy. Whom could they turn to for advice on what to do next—and what would happen to her family now?

Child sexual abuse, like other issues that families and churches need to face in today's world, doesn't wait until we are prepared to face it. The possibility is so terrible that most of us do not want to think about it unless we must, and we may not know where to turn for information and guidance when we need it. This book is written to provide families and churches—and all those in a position to be of assistance to children—with a resource that will help them make a plan to proceed in an unthinkable situation.

The first three chapters provide the basic information someone in Laura's position would need to know. Chapter one looks at the facts of child abuse. The figures so often cited in the media are covered as well as some of the facts and theories that will help parents, families, friends and helpers develop a foundation for understanding the problem. Chapter two addresses the issue of disclosures by children and adults: how to handle them, issues to keep in mind and whom to call for help. Words to use when talking with children and issues to bear in mind will be discussed. Chapter three will provide an outline of what happens next for a family in the midst of a child sexual abuse situation. Often the system's reaction can be as frightening as dealing with the possibility of a child's having been hurt. While specifics will differ from region to region, this overview will help to reassure those who face the situation by providing much needed information about what is ahead and will assist those called upon to help friends, families or parishioners respond. The role of social services, the courts and how an investigation proceeds will be outlined.

Parents, families and friends deal with the tragedy and challenge of child sexual abuse in many different ways. One immediate response often is to reach out and call for help to those they already trust and respect—ministers, Sunday school teachers, lay leaders in their churches, and others who serve in a formal or informal helping ministry. People like Toni Ross, a high school Sunday school teacher at St. Stephen's, and her minister, Alexander Rhodes, didn't expect the news that they received one Thursday afternoon, but they had to deal as best they could.

> *Alexander Rhodes poured himself a cup of coffee and sat down at his desk to review his notes before the meeting of the Christian education commission due to start in fifteen minutes. The knock at the door startled him.*
>
> *"Come on in, Toni," he called to the woman who stood on the other side of the window. "Share a cup of coffee with me before the meeting."*
>
> *"Rev. Rhodes, I didn't know what to do, and I thought I'd better come in early. I'm really glad you were here."*
>
> *Alex smiled supportively and prepared himself for trouble.*
>
> *"You know Albert Jones—he's sixteen and just started coming to my Sunday school class last month. Well, this week I got a call from Tommy Barton's mother—seems that Albert and her six-year-old Tommy were alone in the bathroom during the church service Sunday, and now Tommy says that Albert pulled down his pants and tried to touch his penis. What should I do, Rev. Rhodes? Call the parents, talk to the kids? Tommy's mother is a single parent and has been looking to me for parenting advice for the past few years since Marty died. I feel so responsible. But we were all upstairs in the sanctuary, and no one was even in the bathroom with them—or at least I don't think anyone was. What should we do now? How could God let this happen right in his own house?"*
>
> *How indeed? wondered Rev. Rhodes as he pondered his next step.*

Would you as minister, youth leader, Sunday school teacher or parent know what to do next? Chapter four addresses the response of the church community and ways to proceed that are helpful for families and protect the church from possible negative repercussions. Both the needs of family members dealing with child sexual abuse and the needs of church workers seeking to be of help while dealing with their own responses will be considered. Recognizing that the resources of family and community are frequently not sufficient to deal with all that a family must process and resolve, chapter five considers when therapy is indicated, how to choose a therapist and the course of treatment. Chapter six wrestles with common questions about God's role in tragedy and about good and evil often raised by families and church communities dealing with child sexual abuse in their midst.

For many parents and friends of abused children, issues beyond what to do in the immediate situation become very important once the initial crisis is over. The final chapters look at some common concerns: how God brings healing to children and families and what can be offered (chapter seven), and the long-term impact of child sexual abuse on children (chapter eight). The book closes (chapter nine) with a call for proactive preparation for churches to become abuse-aware congregations and offers steps to take to reduce the risk of abuse on church property or by those ministering to children in the name of the church community, suggesting procedures to have in place before the allegations of abuse arise.

Our God is a redemptive God. Many families who deal with abuse (and quite a few church personnel who have had to walk their congregations through the difficult task of responding to an allegation of child sexual abuse in their midst) can easily agree with the words of Jesus recorded in the Gospel of John when he notes that in the world we will have trouble. But with the healing touch of God, frequently mediated by his people gathered in the local congregation, by the intervention of leadership and the caring of others in the Christian community, I have seen some of the most traumatized come to the point of being able to confess that "in all things God works for the good of those who love him, who have been called according to his purpose" (Rom 8:28)—not that the events themselves were good but that God has brought good out of them. The healing process is never easy or swift. But God is faithful to his people. I hope and pray that this book will be of help to those in need of healing from the impact of child sexual abuse and to those who seek to help them.

1

The Facts

*Developing a Foundation
for Understanding the Problem*

Stacy looked away to hide her shock and to make her face as supportive as possible. Then she turned back toward Mary Jones, the mother of Timmy and Tammy, the seven-year-old twins in her Sunday school class.

"Well, I'm glad you told me, Mary," she said, stalling for time while thinking of a more appropriate response. "Knowing that the twins just told you about being molested by their Uncle Jimmy will certainly be important for me and the rest of the teaching team."

"Can you tell me how they understand what happened to them, or what to expect at their age as a response?" Mary asked, "I'm embarrassed at how ignorant I really am on the topic. I guess you just don't want to believe that it could happen in your home, so you don't really pay attention. I don't even know how common child sexual abuse is or how to help the kids. Maybe I would even have spotted it sooner if I had known what to look for."

"Don't blame yourself," Stacy replied. "Most people really don't know much about the topic." (Myself included, *she thought.)*

How well would you be able to respond to a situation like this? Or if you have responsibility for a Sunday school class or other ministry that touches the lives of young people, how well equipped is your staff to help parents, those who care for children and the young people themselves deal with the complex emotional, physical and spiritual needs of children who have been sexually abused and their families? Could you or your staff respond to the questions Mary asks about basic information? Do you know the frequency or warning signs of child sexual abuse, how children of different ages might understand what happened to them, and how best to help them deal with their experiences?

This chapter builds a foundation of knowledge for those who may have to deal with this issue in ministry situations. First we will focus on an overview of the definition and prevalence of child sexual abuse and how to recognize when it may be occurring. Subsequent chapters deal with specific questions relating to the many ways child sexual abuse impacts children and families and how best to respond in ministry situations.

What Is Child Sexual Abuse?
Any discussion needs to begin with definitions, no matter how difficult they may be. While it is painful to hear from a child that she or he may have been abused, it is next to impossible to know that reality unless we acknowledge its existence and understand what the problem is. The first and most important step in understanding child sexual abuse is admitting to ourselves that this kind of thing occurs in the towns in which we live, in the churches we attend, and in families we know and love. Child sexual abuse is hard to think about, hard to talk about and may even be hard to read about. Yet it must be discussed frankly in order to increase understanding, to help build better protection for children and to train those seeking to help persons impacted by its horror. If the following reading becomes too difficult, take a break and come back later if you need to do so. But we must learn to talk about child sexual abuse because the silence that surrounds it is the molester's greatest ally.

Child sexual abuse may include any kind of sexual act between a child and an adult or between an infant or young child and a significantly older child. Exact definitions may vary slightly from state to state, but the sexual acts may include touching the other's genitalia (by the abuser or victim or both); exposure of the perpetrator's or child's genitalia, including photography or videotaping; requiring a child to view or participate in adult sexual activity; masturbation in front of a child or by rubbing against a child; oral sex by a child to the perpetrator or the perpetrator to a child; and any type of penetration of a child's vagina or anus by a penis, finger or other object. Descriptions such as these conjure up images that evoke a response—anger at perpetrators, fear for children we love, disgust that such events occurs, disappointment in God who allows this to happen, and pain evoked by memories of hurtful sexual experiences. Yet adults who work with children must be willing to face whatever response is engendered within themselves in order to help the children and their families. For some readers, the material discussed in this chapter may bring up powerful emotions or memories. If this is the case for you, please seek the help of a friend, pastor or professional counselor to talk through your response. We cannot effectively help the children we seek to serve if we are still raw from our own pain.

Sexual activities between peers may also be upsetting, but sexual acts are not generally considered child sexual abuse unless there is a significant age difference between the children involved. (The specific legal definitions vary from jurisdiction to jurisdiction, but five years difference is a common yardstick.) Sexualized play that features adult sexual activities (simulating intercourse, for example, as opposed to "Show me yours and I'll show you mine" curiosity), is often a warning sign that one or more of the children involved has been abused. Such play should be taken seriously even if the children are of the same age. Violent, angry or repetitive sex play between peers or children who are nearly the same age, whether entered into willingly or involving coercion of one child by another, should always be taken seriously. Play between the offending children should be stopped or at least closely monitored, and the reason behind such play investigated—even when the play itself does not meet the legal definitions of child sexual abuse.

The vast majority of child sexual abuse occurs in the context of ongoing relationships. It does not require the use of physical force for the coercive abuse of an adult's emotional power over a child to occur. Bribery, playing on fears, trickery and threats of consequences are more typically utilized by an abuser to ensure compliance and silence. These are confusing to children. Telling children that something bad will happen to them if they tell about the touching game or trying to buy them off with gifts may get them to go along with the abuse and to keep quiet for a while, but these techniques can lead to emotional confusion. The violation of trust and innocence often causes more harm than the physical aspects of the abusive experience. This frequently leads to a difficulty in knowing who to trust. Damaged relationships with peers, adults and God become a part of what will have to be addressed by caring adults in the healing process. Knowing how to help can be difficult, since all too often interventions intended to be caring replicate the emotional dynamics of the abusive situation and cause more harm. Later chapters address the specifics of what to consider and how to proceed.

The Scope of the Problem

The sexual abuse of children is not rare. Estimates range from fifty thousand to over a million instances per year in the United States alone. Studies of different groups have come up with a range of figures for the incidence of child sexual abuse, but it is generally agreed that one out of every four females and one out of every seven males has been sexually abused prior to age eighteen. In any group of adults gathered together for ministry or another purpose, 15 to 20 percent of the people present may have been sexually abused by an adult before the age of eighteen. Look around the next time you are at your church for the worship service and think of what these statistics mean to your community.

Most studies show children to be at risk no matter what their ethnic, religious, socioeconomic or family background may be. Children are most often abused by someone they know, and molesters usually increase the severity of their acts against children over time and have more than one victim. No evidence suggests that children who attend church or are reared in Christian homes are immune to the problem. In fact, some aspects of typical Christian child rearing may place these children at higher risk due to having been taught to "be nice"—to respect authority, to trust and obey adults, or to believe that children should be seen and not heard.

Nearly all child advocates, legal authorities and clinical specialists agree that the reported number of instances of child sexual abuse is only the tip of the iceberg, with many more adult-child sexual contacts occurring than those of which authorities are aware. Boys appear to be at less risk of child sexual abuse than girls, but this may be because of the number of incidents that are not reported by boys and their families. Boys may hesitate to tell others for several reasons.

☐ They are socialized to believe that boys are not supposed to be victims.

☐ They fear loss of freedom: if their parents learn what happened in the past or is happening in the present, they will impose more restrictions on their son's activities.

☐ They worry about being thought of as "gay."

☐ Society's double standard sees a preteen girl exposed to adult sexuality as a victim but sees a boy as "getting experience" at a young age.

Parents of all children—whatever their age, sex, race, socioeconomic status, religion or location—must take the threat of child sexual abuse seriously and educate themselves on identification, intervention and prevention techniques whatever the age or sex of their children.

Warning Signs
Often, when parents find out that their children have been or are being abused, they feel guilty that they did not know what signs might have warned them of the danger. Hindsight is always perfect—as any Monday morning quarterback can tell you, after the pressure is over and the rush of the responsibilities of a real-life situation are lifted, it is much easier to see what was not so obvious in the midst of crisis.

If you are looking back now, wondering why you did not see what was happening, remember that even armed with the list of warning signs given below, you might not have discovered what was happening due to efforts that were being made to keep it secret. If you are currently wondering about but have not had confirmation of abuse, the following list may help you to focus your concerns. But be careful not to jump to conclusions. The presence of any—or even most—of these indicators is not conclusive evidence that abuse is occurring. They may be pointing to some problem or concern in a child's life other than child sexual abuse. The definitive answer, unless a child discloses specific details of an abusive experience, is usually best left to a professional—and even the professional may not know for sure. But the presence of the following symptoms may alert you to the need to monitor a child's activities more closely, to pay more attention to his or her relationships with adults or to talk to the child about your concerns. For staff or volunteers working with children, this list may help highlight areas of concern to be discussed with the supervising team in your setting to deal with child abuse situations.

The discussion that follows is organized into physical warning signs, behavioral warning signs, emotional/relational warning signs, physical warning signs and spiritual warning signs. Each section begins with a vignette illustrating the sort of situation that might cause an adult concern about possible child sexual abuse. This is followed by a discussion of warning signs of a particular type. Where different patterns occur for different age groups, they will be highlighted.

Physical Warning Signs

Cheryl opened a can of cat food for Shadrach and sat down for a much-deserved cup of tea. Nursery care had been hectic at Silver Hill Church this morning, and if Mr. Jones hadn't shown up with his daughter and volunteered to stay and help, she didn't know how she would have made it through. Grabbing for the phone with one hand while she poured the hot water with the other, she heard the voice of Lorraine Highly, the mother of two-and-a-half-year-old Kelly.

"Cheryl, I'm glad I caught you at home," Lorraine started. "Kelly was really upset after church today. She told me that her 'wee-wee' hurts and that the 'new man' in the nursery hurt her. I checked her vagina and it's red, like it was rubbed or something. She says it hurts to go to the bathroom too. I hope it's nothing, but I thought you should know."

"I'm glad you called me," Cheryl responded, her cup of tea forgotten. "I'll give Mr. Jones a call and see what might have happened. I'll get back to you with whatever I find out."

Could this be a case of child sexual abuse waiting to be discovered, or has Mr. Jones picked up Kelly by the suspenders of her pants in a misguided effort to play with her and irritated her genital areas innocently? Cheryl knew enough about the physical warning signs of child sexual abuse to know that questions needed to be asked in this situation. The examples that follow will highlight these and other areas of concern.

While the physical signs may seem like the most obvious signs of child sexual abuse, they are often overlooked by parents or caretakers who may not want to be confronted with the unpleasant reality that someone is hurting their child or who may jump to a more mundane conclusion about the source of the problem. These signs are not proof positive, but they should not be overlooked, especially when present in tandem with some of the other categories of signs discussed below.

Torn, stained or bloody underwear may indicate injury or trauma.

Pain, swelling or itching in the genital area, sometimes including a vaginal or penile discharge, may be indicative of infection, irritation or abuse.

Pain in urination or defecation, or urinary or anal bleeding, may indicate an injury secondary to child sexual abuse.

Sphincter control problems may be due to physical damage to muscles in the anal or vaginal areas or may be anxiety-related due to abuse.

Pregnancy and venereal disease, especially among preteens less likely to be involved in consensual sex with peers, obviously may be signs.

Increase in physical complaints such as headaches, stomachaches or abdominal pain may be related to infection or to anxiety symptoms.

Behavioral Warning Signs

"Mrs. Smith," Ricky said, "I like the bathrooms here at the church more than the ones at my daddy's house."

Being an experienced second-grade Sunday school teacher, Karen thought she was ready for just about any answer when she followed up with the question, "Why are they better?"

"Because there are no bathtubs, and no one has to play the slide game. It hurts when my brother and I have to play that."

"What's the slide game?" Karen asked, thinking maybe there was a new toy

out there she hadn't heard of yet.

"It's when my daddy takes a bath with us, and we slide down his legs and hit the stick at the bottom. Sometimes he puts that into our bottoms, and it hurts. I wasn't supposed to tell. Can you keep this a secret?"

What started as an innocent conversation has led down a road that suggests abuse. This boy's comments illustrate both age-inappropriate sexual behavior and the issue of secrecy—common signs of child sexual abuse. (And this underlines why the examples in this section need to be explicit. The children will be explicit when they talk to us about their abuse experiences, and we need to be prepared to listen.)

Behavioral signs that may be indicative of child sexual abuse include the following:

Age-inappropriate sexual behavior. Knowledge of words, sexual activities or role-playing adult sexual encounters may be indicative of having had such experiences. Preschool children may unselfconsciously act out sexual encounters with dolls or in other play situations. Children who are still assisted in toileting or bathing may reveal abuse in these settings by talking about what has been done to a part of their body. In addition to telling with their words, children may also disclose by seeking to initiate behaviors with which other adults have involved them in the past. These may seem "flirty" and cute or be hugely out of place. When a four-year-old girl strokes an adult man's leg and asks, "Do you like it when I touch you there, honey?" she's not trying to be funny or to "come on" to him. She is showing the confusion of intimacy and sexuality that results from other adults introducing her to words and deeds she is too young to understand. (One girl told me in treatment that she touched other men like that because "that's what you do when you like a man"—something her father had taught her.) Family members, friends and those in ministry situations with children need to remember that a child showing these behaviors is not being "promiscuous" but more likely is signaling a need for help.

Use of names for genitalia and other body parts different from those taught at home or used by family may be indicative of having been in a setting where those names were used in an abusive situation. Parents need to correct the use of vulgar or inappropriate language but also need to be on the alert to where their children are learning it and what else may also be happening. This can be done calmly and quietly—"Johnny, you just called your private parts by a different name than we usually use in our family. We usually call a boy's private part his 'pee-pee' but you just used 'wiener.' It's OK to use lots of different names (or 'That's a name I don't like to hear you use,' depending on how you feel about the particular name), but I'm just wondering where you learned that one." This can be easy to overlook, and many adults feel asking questions like the one suggested above is just looking for trouble. But when asked in a quiet and supportive way, such a question may open a door for a child to talk about sexual abuse.

Changes in performance at school. These may be related to wandering thoughts that keep replaying the abusive experience, difficulty concentrating, daydreaming about how to escape from abusive situations, or lack of sleep due to being kept awake at night. A school phobia—sudden dislike or refusal to attend school, or fear of a teacher—likely indicates some sort of dissatisfaction with what is happening there. Being upset when picked up from school may reflect what is happening at home. Either may be indicative of abuse.

Delinquency or running away. For some children this is the only solution to an intolerable home life that includes sexual abuse.

Sleep disturbances. Nightmares, fears of "monsters," bedwetting and difficulty with going to bed may be indicative of sexual abuse. This may be because the abuse occurred in a bedroom or similar setting. Other times it is because memories return and become overwhelming as the child begins to relax and wind down from the daily routine, which allowed him or her to focus attention elsewhere. Sometimes children initially report their experiences of child sexual abuse as dreams or nightmares because they believe that they dreamed them or because they were told by the abuser that the events were not real but only a dream. Parents should listen to the content of dreams that their children talk about with one ear tuned to the possibility that a real event may be being discussed.

Changes in eating patterns. Either a decrease or an increase in food consumption may be a sign. Some people "eat their feelings" when upset, and others are unable to eat at all when worried, frightened or emotionally troubled. A sexually abused child may exhibit either pattern. Trouble with chewing or swallowing (with no apparent physical cause) may be related to replication of the physical motions of a sexual act, recalling the memories.

Emotional and Relational Signs

Ryan always seemed down on himself, distant from the other kids in his middle-school youth fellowship and sickly with frequent headaches and stomachaches. His one good friend was Joe, a popular, self-assured young man who had reached out to him and drawn him into youth group activities. But now Joe was confused; Ryan had told him they couldn't be friends anymore because there were things Ryan was afraid he might tell Joe that would get them all in trouble. Ryan stopped coming to the youth group, and Joe went to his youth group leaders wondering what to do.

Joe knew enough to verify his feeling that something was probably wrong in Ryan's life. Isolation, worry about revealing secrets and sudden withdrawal from emotional intimacy can all be signs of child sexual abuse.

Poor peer relationships. Aggressive acting out or protective withdrawal may be the result of having been sexually abused. Children may become overly assertive to keep potential abusers at a distance, or they may distance themselves from relationships in order not to become close to someone and run the risk of telling the secret that they are not supposed to mention. Some relationships with peers, adults or younger children may become sexualized because intimacy is confused with sexuality due to previous sexualized relationships. Or anger at being abused may be sexualized and acted out toward other children.

Fear of certain formerly comfortable people or places. This fear may arise because of threats made about keeping abuse secret or fear of a repetition of abuse should the child return to that person or place.

Regression. Acting like a younger child or losing recent gains (like toilet training or the ability to sleep the night through in his or her own bed) is one of the ways that a child could signal some sort of emotional trauma, including sexual abuse.

Anxiety-related illnesses. Brought on by the stress of the abuse or the impact of having to keep a secret, some anxiety-related illnesses may include headaches, gastric disturbances, sleep disorders, eating problems and the like.

Secretive talk in relationships. Telling parents or other significant adults that there are secrets that cannot be discussed with them or starting to talk about an issue, then stopping, saying, "I can't tell you about that," may be a sign. Adults can help a child understand the difference between a *secret*— some fact, idea or action that cannot be shared with anyone, and a *surprise*—a planned event where part of the fun is not telling anyone until the moment when they get to find out. *Surprises* are fun, and the whole point is the eventual disclosure of the planned event; *secrets* often involve activities of questionable legal or moral standing, and children should not be made to carry the weight of them. Talk about this in real-life situations, buying presents for Mommy's birthday, for instance, where the adult doing the shopping can emphasize the fun of not telling Mommy for now and surprising her with the gifts later. This can be contrasted with secrets, which often involve breaking rules or doing something wrong that we may be told *not* to tell others but which children should be sure they *do* tell their parents, for protection and so that healing and forgiveness may be brought into the situation.

Poor self-concept. Seeing one's self as bad may be a sign of sexual abuse. Sometimes the offender has prompted the child to violate his or her own sense of what is right and wrong. Or the offender may have told the child that what he or she did was wrong and that the child must not tell anyone about it since he or she would get in trouble for being bad. Children (and adult survivors of child sexual abuse too, for that matter) often have a sense that the problem is deeper than *doing* something bad. They believe that in some sense they have *become* bad by virtue of participation in a forbidden act. Forgiveness rituals appropriate to the child's religious community (prayer, Bible reading, confession and absolution, communion) often help by bringing the reality of God's forgiving grace to bear on the problem.

Depression. Depression may be brought on by child sexual abuse. In addition to feeling bad about oneself, symptoms may include a change in appetite, sleep disturbances, loss of interest in previously enjoyed activities, a feeling of emptiness or sadness, loss of energy, isolating and a wish to avoid life—even, in extreme cases, a desire to be dead. For some children this is related to a feeling of being trapped in the abusive situation and not seeing any way out. These children may feel relief when the story is told. For others, who believe that they are bad and all they do is wrong (perhaps they have been helped to this conclusion by the abuser), telling may create even more problems. It may make them see themselves as someone who can't even be trusted to keep a secret and who gets family or friends in trouble by talking about what should never be voiced.

Signs of decompensation. Children in severe situations may seem to be falling apart psychologically. Symptoms may include inability to function at home or school, suicide attempts and psychotic episodes in which contact with reality is lost. These symptoms are always warning signs that something is seriously wrong in a child's life, and professional help should be found quickly. Sexual abuse is not, however, always the cause. Piecing together the puzzle to determine what the symptoms mean, where they came from and how best to help can be a very difficult task. The assistance of a trained mental health professional is often needed.

Spiritual Signs

"No! Mommy, I won't pray for Uncle Tommy anymore. I don't care if God never helps him to find another job! Besides, prayers don't work anyway. God lets bad things happen, and I don't think he really cares about me anymore!"

Frustration and anger with God can come from many sources; one that is often overlooked is child sexual abuse. When children who have known and loved God begin to turn away from him, the following warning signs should be considered to assess the possibility that abuse has occurred.

Anger at God for "letting bad things happen" is a frequent post-abuse symptom for both children and their families. In children this may be manifest by changes in the way that they talk about God or by refusal to participate in formerly significant religious observances.

Refusal to pray for a specific person. Perhaps the person is the abuser or someone whom the child feels has not been protective. Or the child may respond to the idea of praying for safety or protection with the objection that God doesn't really keep people safe. That can also be a sign. Ask why the child thinks so in order to find out what the concern is, rather than shutting off communication with theological reassurances that God in fact does care. The issue may or may not be child sexual abuse, but the impact on a child's developing faith, in such instances, is serious and should be explored.

"Flight into religion." A child who has been abused may become extremely concerned about the details of religious rites and practices and seek to please God by "getting it right" (excessive time devoted to prayer or Bible study, overly zealous attendance at church functions and so on). While there can and should be solace and healing for an abuse victim in the presence of God and God's people, this is not a healthy drawing near to God but rather a desperate attempt to be perfect so that God will stop the abuse.

Belief that one is uniquely and specially sinful. This is the theological twin of the psychological self-image issue mentioned above. Children who have been abused may see themselves as the most bad, most dirty and most sinful of all people. Biblical verses that offer comfort to people aware of their own sinfulness only elicit an argument that it was not written for them, who are more sinful than even the biblical author could imagine. Such children may believe that they are forever separated from God because of what they did. Instruction, prayer and consistent love are necessary as a response. More about dealing with this reaction to abuse will be detailed in another chapter; for now it suffices to say that this pattern should be recognized as a potential symptom of abuse and not merely treated as a theological error.

Misconstrued theology. A molester may attempt to justify his actions biblically. Because most people abusing children sexually are known to them as respected adults who are a part of their lives, the teachings that they impart have impact. If, for instance, an abuser tells his young victim that God wants fathers (or uncles or teachers) to show kids how special parts of the body can make them feel good, most children would not know that what is presented to them in this way is not God's will. They might go on to conclude that sexual contact between a caring adult and a child is what God has ordained and be quite surprised and resistant when another norm is taught in Sunday school class. Or they might feel rejected when another adult with whom they feel emotionally close is not sexually active with them. The false understandings of God and God's ways need to be corrected gently but firmly, and the root sources of error require careful understanding so that the correction does not cause additional damage.

While all of these signs and symptoms should serve as red flags to warn of the possibility of abuse, none of them in and of themselves is sufficient to give certainty to a parent or caregiver's fears that a child may be in danger. They are listed here to increase awareness of the fact of child sexual abuse and as indicators that may be present in children that we know and love. Like Mary, the mother in the vignette at the opening of this chapter, we may miss the signs of abuse in children in our lives—and when we do, we need to remember the powerful forces at work keeping the abuse a secret and not blame ourselves. But when we, armed with this and other knowledge we may acquire, begin to suspect that a child may be in trouble, we can offer a sanctuary to the children by inviting them to talk about anything that may be on their minds and prepare ourselves and our ministries for the impact of a disclosure. The next chapter will look at the issue of disclosure and what to do to handle the child's needs, the family's needs and the needs of a church or ministry involved with them.

2

Beyond "They Did *What?*"

Recognizing & Dealing with Disclosure

Na'Kisha's eyes filled with tears and her hands trembled as she drew the picture that her Sunday school teacher had requested.

"What's the matter, honey?" Meghan asked. "Are you having a hard time thinking of what to draw for Daddy as a Father's Day card?"

"I'm not gonna draw nothing." Na'Kisha's brow knitted in determination. "I don't like my daddy!"

"Don't be silly, dear. All of your friends are making cards for their fathers. We want to thank them for showing us what God's love is like on earth." Meghan sighed to herself and persisted. Na'Kisha was no longer the easygoing kindergartner she had been at the beginning of the school year.

"But Miss Meghan. He hurts me. I don't want to play his icky touching game anymore. And when he touches my privates, it makes me bleed. Do I have

to make him a card?"

"Of course not, honey," Meghan replied, regretting her earlier assumption
that the root of Na'Kisha's resistance was stubbornness. *"Would you like to talk
more about this in private?"*

"Yes—if I can bring my teddy."

"Teddy can come too."

Disclosures of child sexual abuse intrude into everyday life when and
where least expected. Meghan, in the above example, was planning to
teach a simple lesson on how parents show God's love to children, have
the students make their fathers a card, pray for the needs of her class and
send everyone home. Instead she needs to help Na'Kisha and her family
cope with what may be a horrendous situation. As volunteer or paid staff or
simply as friends or relatives of children, people who interact with young-
sters may find themselves in a similar position. The person who first hears
of a child's distress, as he or she discloses possible abuse, needs to keep in
mind how to help the child, how to ensure the child's safety and how to
deal with the family's reactions. The volunteer or paid staff member needs
to understand his or her role and responsibility in finding out details or
getting others involved—and how to manage his or her own responses to
what has just been disclosed. This chapter addresses what to keep in mind
and what to do when handling disclosures of child sexual abuse.

So much flows through the mind of a person listening to a child when
that child begins to talk about an abusive situation. It is next to impossible
to keep straight what to do to be of the most help to the child and others
involved unless advance preparation has been made. The first and most
important step to take is for churches and agencies to train their workers in
how to handle this eventuality. To whom does the Sunday school teacher,
youth pastor or other person who hears about abuse turn for help? Who
makes the call to the authorities in the case of a mandated reporting situation? How and by whom is the child comforted, protected and cared for?
Are parents or alleged perpetrators notified, and if so, how and by whom?
If the alleged perpetrator is in a ministry position in the church, is she or
he removed from the position pending an investigation or presumed inno-

cent until proven guilty and allowed to continue in ministry?

When the abuse disclosure arises in a family or friendship situation, many equally perplexing questions arise. The needs of the child, the family, the person who hears the story and many others must be kept in balance. Many systems issues with ethical and legal dimensions are raised when one begins to think about how to deal with a disclosure of child sexual abuse. These will be addressed in depth in chapter nine as the issue of proactive preparation is considered. It is to the immediate, practical concerns of how to minister to a child who is disclosing sexual abuse that we turn now.

When You Hear a Disclosure

The working assumption when a child begins to talk about possible abuse needs to be that the child is telling the truth. She deserves to be listened to and believed, at least initially, and allowed to say as much or as little as she wishes to say. The validity of the story can be determined later. At the moment of disclosure, the initial responsibility of the listener is to listen and love. Let the child talk as much she needs, without stopping her to correct or ask detailed questions. Reassure the child that she is still loved and cared for, and that whatever happened is not her fault.

Many abused children have been threatened that something bad will happen to them if they talk. If a child expresses concerns for his own safety or the safety of other family members, reassure him that all that can be done to make sure that he and others are safe *will* be done. Despite what may be an overwhelming desire to make things right and comfort the pain evident in the disclosure, do not make promises that you are not in a position to keep. Assurances such as "Everything will be all right," "I'll make sure no one ever hurts you again" or "God will make sure nothing bad happens anymore" can backfire on the child and the listener if circumstances do not go as hoped for. It can be very difficult for those who work with children to allow them to express their fear or pain without jumping in with a solution, but in cases of child sexual abuse the solutions are often long-term, and the problems cannot be solved with a quick word or action, however well-motivated. The issues that children need to resolve usually center around broken commitments—relationships that should have been safe but have been violated and trust that has been broken. That is why those whom children trust with the privilege of hearing their pain must be especially careful not to set them up for additional trauma by making promises that cannot be kept or offering quick fixes that will not work. It is better for the child, though more difficult for the listener, to reflect the pain ("I know this must be so hard for you"), offer reassurances of which they can be sure ("Whatever happens, God will be with you and see you through") and help the child deal with the emotions that accompany telling the story.

Young children, as in the example given at the beginning of this chapter, frequently tell about child sexual abuse when they are being hurt and want the pain to stop. They often have no idea of the full implications of telling their story or of its impact on those around them. Their stories may emerge unselfconsciously and in the normal course of events—interrupting a class activity or school outing when least expected. They may hesitate when they remember that they have been warned not to tell. Their motivation to keep the secret is usually related to the consequences with which they have been threatened if they talk, or to loyalty to the abuser, or to a genuine desire to be a "good" boy or girl and do what they have been told. They may have a sense of the "badness" of the sexualized activities they have participated in without understanding why others might think it wrong. It is especially important, therefore, that the listener not respond judgmentally or (though feeling it) show horror in a way that would make the children think that *they themselves* are the object of disapproval or revulsion. If the listener cannot keep his or her emotions from becoming visible, the emotions should be labeled and attributed to something other than the child. "I'm feeling angry that someone would hurt you, Johnny, and that's why I seem upset" will go a long way toward calming the preschooler who, because of his or her stage of development, normally expects that he or she is the cause of whatever emotion is elicited in the adult—and expects to be blamed for making an adult feel bad.

Children's fears expressed while they are telling of their abusive experiences or shortly afterward must also be taken seriously. A child who finishes a narrative of his or her abusive experiences and then asks "Is my

Mommy dead now?" or "Is that noise the rhinoceros coming to eat me?" may be voicing a fear based on a threat by the molester who warned of what might happen if the truth was told. In a calm voice that takes the fear seriously without endorsing it, reassure the child that he or she need not worry about that and that you will help to keep him or her safe and get people who can help. If the fear is something that you are certain that you can safely contradict, it is all right to do so. (For instance, the boy who says "You hate me now, and I will go to hell for telling Uncle Freddy's secret" can be reassured that the listener does not hate him, despite what he may have been told to believe, nor will God send him to hell for telling the truth about a harmful thing that was done to him.) But, as mentioned above, care must be taken not to promise things that cannot be delivered.

As children get older (in the elementary school years), they are more aware of the "wrongness" of sexual abuse and more likely to keep the secret because of shame. Or they may fear that they will be thought badly of. They do not wish to be thought of as different or bad compared with their peers and are less likely to talk about something that they know sets them apart. They are also more likely to understand the implications of telling. Often the abuser emotionally or financially supports the family, and the child does not want to cause this person—the stepfather or uncle or aunt or older brother—to get in trouble, because removal of this person would cause problems (reduced income or other changes in life circumstances) for the family. Children feel a conflict between their desire to tell about the abuse and get it to stop and their sense of responsibility to the family that pushes them to sacrifice their own well-being for what they believe is the family's good. This often leads to a child's attempting to cover up telltale signs of abuse with plausible stories that might account for the symptoms noted. Or when a disclosure has been made, it is often retracted when the cost to the child or family is made clear. This is important to remember when the alleged abuser is a friend, church leader or member of the minister's family. We are likely to want to believe that the retraction came out of a desire to tell the truth; we want to believe that no abuse took place. While this is possible, when a retraction occurs, asking oneself why a child is changing the story *now* is more helpful than automatically assuming that the initial story was false and the latter one true—no matter how comforting that may be to the listener or broader church community. Often the reason is more rooted in seeking to avoid unpleasant aftereffects of telling than in a sudden desire to tell the truth.

When teenagers disclose a history or current situation of sexual abuse, it is most often in the context of a caring relationship with an adult with whom trust has been built. They may confide in a youth leader because of the weight of guilt that they carry, wanting to be prayed for and released from the perceived burden of their sin. In that case, pray for them, assure them of God's forgiveness, and then help them to see that they were not to blame. Don't start with the intellectual argument of who is at fault and why, or they may see you as just one more adult who did not listen or understand. Some teens are shocked to hear themselves open up with their story of abuse and find themselves saying more in the intimacy of close relationships than they had intended. They may seek to swear the adult who hears to secrecy and ask for their confidentiality to be respected. The importance of what they have disclosed should be stressed and no confidentiality offered for the potentially dangerous abusive situation. Beware of giving in to the temptation of promising confidentiality before you know what topic you will be discussing. A request "Will you promise to never tell anyone what we talk about?" needs to be responded to with carefully chosen words such as "Julie, most things that kids tell me I can keep secret, but sometimes, when safety is involved, I have to talk to other people. I hope that you can still tell me what is on your mind and trust me to do what I think is going to help you the most."

Older children (late elementary and teenage) may also knowingly misrepresent the truth for the shock value of exaggeration or to get someone in trouble. Again, the first response must be to believe them. Then, if a story does not hold together, it may be necessary to go back to them later and ask what was going on that they distorted the truth. Children who lie and allege sexual abuse wrongly may not have been abused, but they certainly have serious problems that need adult attention if they are capable of planning and implementing such a deception.

In summary, the adult who hears a disclosure from a child will ideally have thought about this possibility beforehand and have a plan in mind. The working assumption will be to believe the child at least initially. Being careful not to make promises that cannot be kept, the hearer will seek to identify fears and reassure when possible, working to keep the child safe. While doing all this, the adult will begin to consider what to do next.

What to Do After Hearing a Disclosure

This chapter has focused so far on what to keep in mind while hearing a sexual abuse disclosure from a child. This section will consider what to *do*.

The initial action that needs to be taken is to *assess the safety of the child* and take whatever steps necessary to make sure that he or she is not at immediate risk of harm in retaliation for disclosure. Should the incident involve intervention during or immediately after a sexual assault, this may involve providing emergency medical care or arranging transport to an urgent care medical center. In the absence of open wounds, bleeding or other physical symptoms that clearly necessitate medical attention, the person hearing the account of the sexual trauma should undertake an informal safety assessment before determining the next steps to take. This assessment should include finding out, from the child and possibly others in the child's family, the answers to the following questions.

With whom will the child be going home? Is that person the alleged perpetrator? Does the perpetrator named by the child live in the house or have immediate access to the child (the next-door neighbor, the grandmother who comes over to visit daily)? The issue to be determined here is how great the risk is that the child will be abused again or retaliated against for telling. If a child tells you about having been touched inappropriately by Daddy's business partner who lives in another state and who is not currently in the area, the degree of risk is lower than if he or she tells of something having happened with a babysitter who lives down the street.

Who else knows about the alleged abuse? The purpose of this question is twofold. First, you will find out who is available to the child already as a support system to help cope with what has happened and with the changes that having told will bring. Second, you will see if a parent or guardian is already aware. If so, a comment to the adult responsible for the child—

mentioning that the child has told you about the alleged abuse and you are available to help the family—may be appropriate. It depends on whether or not the responsible adult is the alleged perpetrator, how stable he or she is emotionally at the time, and how the child reacts to the idea that you need to talk to this person. If the parent or guardian is not aware, you may need to pass on what the child has revealed to you, indicate your desire to support and be available, and let him or her know what other actions you may be taking. In the case of an institutional setting such as a church or school, internal protocol should spell out who is responsible for handling the various aspects of this situation so that the hearer does not feel alone and unsupported in struggling with issues that he or she may not be prepared to address. The child may also identify other children who are aware of the abuse or are victims themselves. If this occurs, it may be necessary to reach out to them with help as well.

Is there a history of irrational or unsafe behavior on the part of the parent or guardian or others who have access to the child? This question addresses how the parents or guardians of a child will respond when told of the alleged abuse revealed by their child. Friends or church-family members of the parents may know them well enough to be fairly sure that they will react with caring concern and support. Or they may know that they are more likely to become emotionally overwhelmed and to act unpredictably. More safeguards to protect the child and more support for the parent or guardian need to be put in place in the second instance. While we can never be sure how an adult will react to the news of his or her child being molested, histories that indicate substance abuse, mental illness or previous erratic behavior are of concern.

What does the child think will happen next now that he or she has told about what occurred? With this question you are seeking to understand the child's fears or concerns, as well as hoping to get an insight into the working of the family system to which the child will be returning. A response such as "I'll get a whipping for sure" is a red flag for danger, while a more reflective "I think Mommy will cry and say she is sad I got hurt" indicates a more benign situation. If the fear or concern the child expressed is unlikely or impossible, the child can be reassured on the spot. For instance, children may feel that God doesn't love them anymore because of what happened or that they can't come back to youth group once the leader knows their secret. God's love and forgiveness can be discussed and modeled by a compassionate and sincere response. If the fear or concern is beyond the control of the hearer, children should be reassured that all that can be done to keep them safe will be done. And they should be encouraged with prayer or Scripture verses: remind them that "nothing can separate us from the love of God" or that "Jesus has promised to be with us always, even to the end of time." Pat answers must be avoided—the pain that children feel is real, and their fears can be overwhelming. False reassurances that do not pan out can undermine their faith at a time when they will need it the most. But reminders of the truths of God can give them a foundation to stand on as they deal with the aftermath of having disclosed child sexual abuse.

Can you—or someone you can help the child identify—be available as a support person? By the end of a brief conversation with a child, it may be clear that good support is available through the parents, extended family or family friends. But if the child has not mentioned someone who will help through this time, it is a good idea to ask who the child can talk to about how he or she is feeling and who can help if needed. Depending upon your relationship with the child and the family, it may or may not be appropriate to offer to be of help yourself. Remember, though, not to offer more than you can realistically do. Unkept promises in abuse situations can retraumatize children as they find out that yet another adult whom they thought they could count on turns out not to be there for them. Adults who make those promises usually are seeking to meet a real need a child has. But they may overcommit in response to a question like "Will you make sure I'm safe if my Mommy gets mad?" rather than giving a careful pledge to be of help that recognizes the limits of what they can do. Watch out for this trap. Be aware that it will be difficult to handle the emotions you feel amidst this situation with a needy child. It is better to give the realistic answer even if it seems inadequate ("I can't be with you all the time to make sure you are safe, but I will try to find someone who can help you and your family, and I will pray for you every day") because it gives the child something real to rely upon.

If you don't feel it is safe for the child to go home with the parent or adult guardian who brought him or her, you need to call the police. In most jurisdictions only the police or a social service agency staff person with specific legal authority to do so may hold a child against the parent's wishes. The best approach is to go directly to the police, who can move quickly to ensure a child's safety and who have the authority and training to make quick and decisive interventions. As hard as calling in outside help may be, if there is any doubt about a child's safety, it must be done. And, if the hearer is a mandated reporter (a member of one of those professions required by law to report suspicion of child abuse to the child protective services agency in their state), if the abuse response protocol of the church or agency requires, or if the child or family requires the support and protection of official involvement, a report to the child protective services must be made. (The filing of such a report and the actions and reactions the report sets into motion will be the subject of the next chapter.)

Lets see how all this looks by imagining the conversation that Na'Kisha and Meghan might have in private following the classroom event described at the beginning of this chapter.

"Miss Meghan, I'm scared," Na'Kisha told her teacher. "I wasn't supposed to tell about the touching game. Do you think I'll get in trouble now?"

"I'm not sure what will happen, honey," Meghan replied, "but I think you did the right thing by telling about it. I will try to help you. Can we ask God to help too?"

"OK."

"Oh God, I thank you for Na'Kisha—for her smile and joy and laughter— and for her bravery in telling about what happened with her father. Be with her and her family now, we pray. Help her to know that nothing can separate her from your love and that you will always be with her. And be with us as we talk more now, in Jesus' name."

"Amen."

"Na'Kisha, I need to ask you some important questions now. Does anyone else know about this touching game?"

"Only my daddy 'cause he was there. I never told anyone else."

"And who brought you here to church today, your mommy or your grandmother?"

"Both. My weekend at Daddy's is next week, and Grandma came 'cause we're going to Uncle Joe's after church for a picnic."

"What do you think will happen now that you told?"

"I think Daddy will be mad, but Mommy and Grandma will be proud of me for telling the truth even when it's hard."

"I'm proud of you too. Now you go back to class and play with your friends until snack time. I need to talk to Mrs. Smith, the Sunday school director, and then she and I will probably need to talk to your mother. You did a good job talking to me about hard stuff."

"OK, Miss Meghan," Na'Kisha said as she skipped back to class. "Don't be too long, or you'll miss the chocolate chip cookies."

From this brief example (admittedly a best-case scenario for teaching purposes) you can see how the hearer (Meghan) was able to reassure the child of God's love and of her continued support. With just a few questions she found out that Na'Kisha's father would not be seeing her again until the next weekend, that her mother was accompanied to church by the girl's grandmother and would have support when told the story, and that Na'Kisha expected that her mother and grandmother would be supportive. Meghan ended the time with Na'Kisha by sending her back to the classroom and headed off for a consultation and planning session with the director of Sunday school to consider how to proceed. She was careful to let Na'Kisha know what to expect next.

Assuming that the safety issue has been dealt with as suggested above, the next most immediate question is: *How and by whom should the parent or guardian be informed of what the child said?* In the case where the person in whom the child confides is a friend or family member, most often that person will be the one to talk to the parent. In an institutional setting like a church, school or social agency, the written protocol for management of abuse-related issues should spell out how to handle this. Usually the person who heard the allegations will let the parents or guardians know with the help of a supervisor or another trained person to assist in the formulation of the message and to support the hearer in the telling of the story. If there is no known danger to the child likely to arise from telling the parent or guardian, the person should take a direct and matter-of-fact approach. It is important to be aware that the issue is very difficult to hear about concerning one's own child and that the parent will need support to deal with what is said. The initial reaction may be shock, denial or a desire for more information than is available at the moment. The parent or guardian enters unknown ground in this area and needs as much information as the informing person can give as to what will happen next both on the part of the church, school or friend and on the part of those who may need to be notified. A well-defined protocol of response to child sexual abuse (in an institutional setting) or a carefully thought-out plan (in a family or friendship setting) will give the first, and the next chapter will provide information to help give the second.

Let's return to Meghan and Mrs. Smith, the Sunday school director, as they talk to Na'Kisha's mother, Ms. Jones.

"Was Na'Kisha OK in class today, Miss Meghan?" Ms. Jones asked. "You look like something's wrong."

"It's just that she told us something upsetting. May we speak with you a moment privately?" Meghan replied.

"Of course. 'Kish, go wait with Grandma upstairs while I talk to your teachers, OK?"

"Thanks for taking the time to talk with us," Meghan began. "Na'Kisha's class was making Father's Day cards today, and she told us something about her father you should know. She said that he touched her private parts and that it hurt her when he did."

"No! I had no idea! That's awful! What did she say? How did it come up?"

"She said she didn't want to make a card for him. We don't know much about it, but we wanted you to know. She said she never told anyone—and that she thinks that you and your mother will be proud of her for telling the truth even when it's hard."

"Of course we are. But I'm not sure how to help her. What should I do next? Frankly, I'm worried that I might make it worse for her by how I react."

"The most important thing right now is to believe her," Mrs. Smith replied, *"Let her know that you are not mad at her—in fact, you are proud just like she expected. And tell her that you will work at keeping her safe so no one hurts her anymore."*

"We have a protocol planned out for how to help families in this situation," Meghan continued, *"and the next step is for us to confer with the minister. Then one of us will call the child protective services hotline. They should contact you within a day or two. She told us she is not scheduled to see her father until next weekend?"*

"That's right."

"Then just treat her as normally as possible. If she brings it up, listen without trying to pump her for details. Assure her that she did the right thing by telling. And if you need help, call us. You have my number at home in the handouts from the beginning of the Sunday school year. I want to be of assistance to you and to Na'Kisha as you walk through this."

As you can see, the approach was direct. The facts were presented with no embellishment, and no apology was made for not knowing everything about what happened after only a brief time with the child. Ms. Jones was told what to expect next, given some input on how to help her daughter, and offered specific help.

Suppose the answers had not been so benign:

"What do you think will happen now that you told?"

"I'll get in trouble. Mommy told me not to tell, 'cause she needs Daddy's money 'til she starts her new job, and she won't get any if he goes to jail."

In this very different situation it would be important to consult immediately with the person who supervises and coordinates abuse response for the church. The police would likely need to be called immediately if Na'Kisha's story was accurate—if her mother knew about the abuse and was not being protective of her. Most likely a decision would be made not to tell her mother about the call until after the police arrived; if she were to try to take Na'Kisha and leave the church building, staff would have no authority to hold her there. Or depending on the situation, if a member of the church staff had a good relationship with the mother and could convince her of the need to talk to the police and child protective services, another route might be taken to ensure the child's safety.

A final consideration in managing the immediate response to a disclosure of child sexual abuse is *meeting the needs of others involved.* In a school, church or institutional setting this may include other children who heard what was said, the adult to whom the disclosure was made, and other staff who are involved. In a family or friendship situation the more diffuse needs of the others who are aware and involved need to be considered.

Other children do not need to know the details of what may have been alleged. Depending upon their ages they may have questions about what was brought up in their hearing, but these can be addressed by saying simply that their classmate says she has been hurt by someone and that the grownups are helping her with her problem. It is possible that another child present may have been abused or that his or her own feelings of being unsafe or at risk due to another issue might be activated by hearing about this child's trauma. Staff should be alert to this possibility and be on the lookout for children who seem upset. Comfort them with the statement that it is sometimes hard to hear about a friend being hurt. Ask them what their peer said that disturbs them. Try to pinpoint the area of their concern and assist in formulating a response to help them to deal with their fears.

Other children in families also need some kind of general explanation of what is going on, especially if they see the adults in their world upset and angry. A brief statement is usually enough for the moment—something along the lines of "Somebody hurt your sister, but we are taking care of it to make sure that she is safe—and you too. Don't worry about it now and let the adults take care of it for today." If a child abuse report is made, it is likely that other children in the family will be interviewed at some time, and the professionals involved can provide further input.

Family members, friends or staff at churches or schools often need support in dealing with their own feelings that are aroused by the allegations. These may be feelings from their own past—echoes of their own abusive experiences or times when they have not been protective of others—or concerns about current issues that they can no longer push into the background when confronted with the enormity of the abuse allegations made. A first step is to simply acknowledge with them the presence of these feelings. A second step is to provide an emotionally safe place and a skilled person to listen and help them process what has happened. In a church this can sometimes be accomplished by a professionally led discussion or two to talk about what is happening and to help the minister screen for those who may have deeper issues that need individual follow-up. In a school this may be teacher or support staff meetings to let feelings and concerns be voiced. Family members often need to talk to one another or to an outside professional. Allegations of abuse do not happen in a vacuum.

Regardless of the setting, an important next step is to keep those involved abreast of developments—what has happened and what will happen next. Rumors fly at a time of crisis, and some kind of damage control is often necessary. Unnecessary fears or undeserved resentments about things allegedly said or done that never actually occurred can be avoided with proper management of critical information. (Think in advance about the "how-to's" of doing this. You will be wise to have a plan in place long before it is needed. More on this in chapter nine.)

Finally, others in the community or family may not know how best to respond to those whose family has been rocked by child sexual abuse allegations. In seeking to be nonintrusive and cautious about interfering, they more often than not leave the family feeling unsupported and overwhelmed at a time when practical and emotional support is greatly needed. Offering to run errands, cook meals or clean house could be of great help to a family overwhelmed by what has just happened to them. Suggesting a specific time ("I'm free from one to three on Thursday, what can I do to help then?") or task ("I'm doing my grocery shopping Monday night. Would it help if I did yours then too?") is more helpful than a general "Call me if you need help," which may be seen as insincere or half-hearted. It may take weeks for a family to recover enough to assume any kind of normal functioning after a disclosure of child sexual abuse, and the church community should support them without feeling that the family is malingering and ought to be getting over it sooner. Even after the immediate shock of discovery is over, the family will need tender loving care for the next few months as its members progress through the steps described in the next chapter—as the child protective service, police and judicial systems step in and react to the allegations made.

3

What Happens Next?

Understanding the Systems Involved

Rev. Steve Lee smiled at Mrs. White across the desk and assured her that she and her daughter Marie could stay in his office until the social worker arrived. The child protective worker had agreed to interview the family at the church rather than in their home, since they felt safer there.

"I've worked with Margarita Ruiz before. She will be fair and thorough."

"But what happens next? I'm so scared."

"Of course you are. You don't know what to expect from the system," Steve replied. "Let me try to prepare you for the steps that are ahead. Of course, each case is different, but the general flow is the same. You and your family will be interviewed by the child protective services and by the police. The situation may or may not end up in either family court or criminal court or both. It can be confusing, but your church family will stand beside you all of the way."

One of the most frightening aspects of managing child sexual abuse for families and those who walk through the time of trial with them, both professionals and friends, is the sudden involvement in a world of unknown procedures and unclear expectations. It can seem that everyone else on the playing field knows all the rules and probable outcomes, and the child and family and their supporters barely even know what game is being played. This chapter explores the role of the various systems and procedures involved in a typical child sexual abuse scenario—from the initial call to the child abuse hotline or police department to the final placement or adjudication. As noted in the opening vignette, every case is a little different. While general procedures are the same, specifics may vary a little in different jurisdictions and according to each family's special circumstances. This overview will provide a working knowledge of what can be expected. Obtaining legal counsel or building relationships with the people involved in the child sexual abuse evaluation and adjudication process in a particular community can fine-tune your expectations to what will happen in your own locale.

Making the Initial Call to Child Protective Services

The previous chapter discussed disclosure of child sexual abuse and left the reader poised to make a call to the child protective services agency in their jurisdiction. Several questions should be decided prior to making the call. First, the person who has knowledge of the alleged abuse must know if he or she is a mandated reporter of child abuse. If not, then the decision of if and when to report the alleged abuse is made according to one's own moral code and whatever one believes is best for a child and family. A family member who hears about child abuse in a cousin's household, for instance, may be motivated by a desire to protect the child, to help the family or to bring sin to light so that the forgiveness of God and eventual reconciliation may come to pass. But there is no legal mandate that he or she must report the situation to authorities. A mandated reporter, on the other hand, is under specific legal obligation to report knowledge or suspicion of child abuse to the proper authorities within a specific time limit and in a specified way.

Each jurisdiction has legally defined who is a mandated reporter within their state. People with a professional service relationship to children are included in the list—teachers, doctors, mental health professionals, dentists and the like. Most states include clergy as mandated reporters. Some exclude clergy. Others require a report to be made unless the knowledge of the alleged abuse was obtained "in the context of confession." Clergy need to be aware of the laws in their state. For those who do not know, the state office of the attorney general is a good starting point to find out. Various presbyteries and denominations have taken different stands on how far the reporting requirement should extend within a church. Do all staff fall under the mandate? All volunteers? Again, it is wise to consult your local church organization to see how this has been handled in your area. For the safety of children, it is better to have all staff required to report abuse— either to the authorities directly, in consultation with the clergy or their designated representative, or to senior clergy or lay staff who will make the reporting decision for the church or organization. Whatever policy is decided upon should be written up, made available publicly and followed without exception in all cases that meet reporting criteria.

The state hotline for child abuse is often a toll-free number. Some areas have separate numbers for mandated and nonmandated calls. If yours does, try to call the right one for your situation. If you call the wrong number, you will be referred to the right one and can call again, but you will have wasted time. The person making the actual call to the child protection authorities should keep written notes, including the number called, the date and time of day, the name of the person spoken to, and the general content of what has been reported. You should also ask if there is a case or record number for the call in case you need to follow up later. Some states now tape all calls to the hotlines for record-keeping purposes.

If you have a copy of the follow-up written form that mandated reporters need to file after making the phone call to the reporting line, fill it out before you call, and you will have answers ready for the questions that you will be asked. Copies can be obtained from a local child protective services office. It is better to have these forms before you need them rather than scrambling to get them in order to meet the legally imposed deadline for filing in writing within twenty-four to seventy-two hours of the call (depending on jurisdiction).

You can expect to be asked the name and birth date (or age) of the child alleged to have been abused, his or her home address and current location, names and birth dates (or ages) of siblings or other children in the house, names and birth dates (or ages) of adults living in the house, the circumstances of the alleged abuse, how you heard about it and from whom, what evidence you have to support your suspicions, and if you know of any previous abuse. If you know of additional information that may be helpful to the child (she's really frightened of unknown men, so try to send a woman investigator) or to the worker (the stepfather raises German shepherds and has been known to let them roam free around the yard to ward off unexpected visitors), you should notify the person taking down the information at that time. Some child protective departments collect demographic information too—such as the race or ethnic group of the child. Give as much information as you have but don't delay making the call simply because you don't have all the data.

If you are a mandated reporter, you should give your name and the name of your organization, agency, school or church. In most jurisdictions an effort will be made to keep this information confidential at least at the early stages of the investigation, though it may need to become public at a later point if a trial becomes necessary. You may decide to tell the family of the child who is alleging abuse that you are making a report. Often it is a good idea to do so if you hope to have an ongoing relationship with the family and are available to walk them through the process of dealing with the allegations and investigations. Clinicians and clergy often feel that the trusting relationship that they have built with families requires that they tell them when it has become necessary to make a report to the child protective agency, but there is no legal requirement to do so. A family can often guess who made the report—especially if there is only one person that they have told about the allegations. If you made the report as a part of your professional role with good intentions based on reasonable suspicion, you are immune from criminal or civil prosecution from the person or persons about whom you filed a report. If you are a mandated reporter and do not make a report, there is likely to be provision in your local law for a fine and possible jail time upon being found guilty of not reporting—and also a liability for civil suit from the child and his or her family to recover the cost of damages done to them by the alleged abuser after you knew about the abuse and should have reported it (because it would presumably have stopped).

The weight of the responsibility of making a mandated reporter's call to the child protective services can be very heavy. Many people find themselves trying to guess which would be better: to make the call and get authorities involved or to see if the family can handle it on its own, perhaps with church support. Someone who is not a mandated reporter has this option, but for the mandated reporter the choice is clear. We are legally required to make the call as soon as we have a suspicion that abuse is occurring or may have occurred. Not only is the mandate legally compelling, but the making of such a call is consistent with Christian belief in justice and protection for the helpless. In order for healing to begin, the problem must be brought into the light so that children can be protected, sin exposed and confessed, and God's redemptive powers brought to bear on the situation.

The Response of the Child Protective Service Agency

Once a report has been received by the hotline operator, a legally mandated clock is ticking. Within a specified period of time—usually not more than forty-eight to seventy-two hours—investigation workers must start the process of deciding the validity of the allegations. They will meet with the child and family involved, and they may seek out the reporter for more information about what has been alleged. If there is evidence that a crime has occurred, the child protective services will also report the incident to the police so that a criminal investigation can begin. The speed of their response and the action taken, if any, depend on their assessment of three critical factors:

☐ Is the child in immediate danger and in need of removal from the home? Immediate danger may require transport to a hospital or medical facility for treatment of wounds or trauma, or removal to a foster care setting if the guardians cannot keep the child safe.

☐ Is the child in short-term danger requiring protective interventions? If the family cannot keep the child safe—perhaps because of substance abuse on the part of the guardian or perpetrator, or because of fear of violence from the alleged abuser—then the child may be placed with a relative or in a community foster home for his or her protection.

☐ Is the child safe at the moment, but does the family need supportive services to reduce the risk of abuse in the future? Then the child may stay in the home while a case is opened and community resources are put into place.

Staff is limited, and the need is great. Sometimes the circumstances force investigators to prioritize, and a case that seems of crucial importance to the person making the report and to the family involved may take a back seat to a situation of more immediate danger. When you are involved with helping a family in that situation, encourage them to be patient while awaiting a visit from the investigation team. It is also helpful to call again to follow up if no contact is made—street names can be misread, messages erased from phone machines or notes left on the door removed by someone who does not want contact made. A follow-up call can help keep a family from being labeled noncooperative when, in fact, a communications slip-up prevented the contact.

In addition to talks with the investigator, the initial investigation stage of the child protective services involvement may include several other recommendations. While it is possible for a parent to refuse to follow the suggestions of the protective services worker in the absence of a court order, the recommendations are generally made in the hopes of collecting more information and seeing what the child's needs are at the present time (as well as seeking to understand more fully what happened to him or her in the past). They should be followed unless the parent has overwhelming reason to feel that they are not good for the child or family. If that is the case, the parent may talk with the supervisor or refuse the intervention. The matter will come before a family court judge if the protective services staff feel that the issue is important enough to push that far. Recommendations may include a *sexual abuse medical examination*, a *diagnostic interview* with a mental health professional, and possibly a *psychiatric interview* for one or more family members.

A *sexual abuse medical examination* is a specialized exam undertaken by trained medical professionals to look for evidence that abuse may have occurred. It uses techniques that have been proven to be successful, following methodologies that will hold up in court. The medical professional will want to talk to the parent or guardian, talk to the child and examine the child following a specified protocol that systematically reviews possible injury or trauma. This may include an examination of the vaginal or anal regions with a colposcope—a tiny tube with a light that is inserted in the anus or vagina and allows the medical professional to view the interior walls looking for injury. The presence or absence of injury or scarring, as well as the specific pattern of location of the injuries, may help to determine the exact nature of the trauma (whether there was penetration of the vagina or anus; whether the damage was done by a finger, penis or hard object), the time elapsed since the assault (estimated by the healing that has occurred in the traumatized areas) and the frequency of the assault (estimated by the presence of differentially healed areas). The colposcope is often equipped to allow for the taking of pictures of the injured areas for use as evidence if a criminal trial follows the investigation.

Families often wonder whether or not their own medical consultants can do these investigations. This is a complicated question that needs to be addressed on a case-by-case basis. Not all medical professionals are trained in the exacting procedures necessary to collect information that potentially is evidence in a criminal trial. Nor do all have the equipment needed. Doing an anal or vaginal exam on a child who may already have been sexually traumatized requires knowledge of developmental issues, family dynamics and interview techniques that even the best pediatrician or family practitioner may not have been trained in. Finally, prior knowledge of a family can be a complicating factor. The evaluator who already knows the child or others in the family may be able to put them at ease or approach issues in a culturally sensitive manner, but the tradeoff is that he or she may bring previously formed judgments about the child or family to bear that cloud the issue at hand. Someone who has known the family for years may have trouble believing that Uncle Henry, whom they have known since he was a baby, may in fact be a molester. Or they may have felt that something was off with the family for decades and be just a little too eager to find evidence that would finally confirm their long-held hunches. Generally it is best for a stranger to conduct this interview, though consultation with a medical professional who knows the family well may be a helpful adjunct to the investigative process, either through conversations with the person conducting this exam or by input to the others on the investigatory team.

Parents and families of children who may have been abused often have mixed feelings about having their children subjected to an exam that may reawaken feelings of traumatization through what can be viewed by the child as intrusive and scary procedures. While these feelings are understandable, it is important to go forward with this procedure when there is reason to believe that it may provide helpful information. Doing so is advisable for several reasons:

☐ Children do not always tell all that has happened to them, and a child that acknowledges only being touched on the buttocks may in fact be revealed by the exam to have suffered further trauma that needs medical or psychological attention.

☐ Children frightened by the abusive experience or abused in their sleep or in the dark may not know all of what happened. They may report that they were touched on the inner thigh and urinated in their sleep (because they remember feeling wet), but the information gained medically may show penetration that suggests that the liquid they felt was blood or semen. Again, this information is helpful for planning treatment for the child and may impact the criminal case against the alleged offender.

☐ The findings of a thorough exam may also rule out some fears or concerns and put a parent's mind at ease. Going through the exam with a trained, sensitive and supportive medical professional may reassure the child that he or she is really OK in areas that the child believes were somehow damaged when he or she was hurt there. The interaction with a skilled professional may allow the child and family an opportunity to ask questions and receive answers to previously unvoiced fears or concerns.

The person conducting this exam knows how difficult it is for the child and the family and will do everything possible to help minimize the trauma and shame.

A *diagnostic interview* with a mental health professional is also frequently a part of the investigatory process. A specially trained worker with knowledge of child development, skilled in relating to children and making them feel comfortable while discussing difficult issues, and equipped with interview techniques age-appropriate for children from two to sixteen, will meet alone with the child for one or more sessions with the goal of helping the child talk about what happened, so that the investigation team, parents and treatment providers can have a clear picture of what occurred and where to go next. Information from these interviews will help the child protective services worker decide what interventions to recommend for the family and will provide the police and prosecutor with data as they wrestle with whether to take the case to court or not. Sometimes these assessments may be "blind"—that is, the interviewer is not provided with information about the child's allegations prior to the meeting so that there is no possibility of leading the child. Whatever comes out of the session comes out of the child alone. Other times the mental health professional plays a synthesizing role in the investigation process, going into this interview with all of the data already collected by the team and seeking to clarify and augment what is already known.

Typically this interview consists of several stages. The interviewer will spend a few minutes with the child helping him or her feel comfortable, often interacting over a neutral activity such as coloring or playing with puppets or a game. Depending on the age of the child, this initial phase may also be used to assess the child's communication abilities and to look for knowledge of concepts (over-under, in-out, up-down), time and place, colors and other information that may be important in the telling of the story of the alleged abuse later in the interview. The child's ability to distinguish between truth and a lie is assessed and an age-appropriate commitment to tell the truth obtained. The interviewer also assesses the style and pattern of a child's communications. Does he or she generally make eye contact, answer in one word or complete sentences, talk freely or seem to have canned responses, consistently agree or disagree with adult statements, or predictably answer only yes or no to all questions, regardless of what is asked? These and other variables that will be important to an accurate understanding of the child's statements in later phases of the evaluation can be assessed informally during this initial "play" component while the child is becoming acclimated to the interviewer.

Parents or guardians are not usually included in the interview. With younger children or children who are especially frightened by the prospect of talking to a stranger about the alleged abuse, parents or guardians are sometimes invited to sit in on the initial phases of the interview. This can help make the child more comfortable. As he or she sees the parent interacting normally with the interviewer, the child realizes that it is OK to talk to this person. Parents or guardians may also be asked to tell the child that it is OK to talk about the alleged abuse with the interviewer. If the parent or guardian is ill at ease or seems unable to encourage the child to talk about what happened, the parent or guardian's presence in the interview would be counterproductive, and he or she will not be invited in. Even when parents are totally appropriate in their handling of the situation, children often shield their parents from aspects of what happened to them and are more likely to be forthcoming and complete in telling all the details of their experience if their parents are not in the room. The interviewer may also be following an established protocol so that all children interviewed are treated exactly the same and may have elected never to have parents or guardians come into the interview so as not to make some interviews different from others.

When the child appears to be comfortable, the interviewer will move on to inviting him or her to talk about the alleged abuse. Depending upon the child's age and developmental level, this portion of the interview may involve talking, playing or some combination of the two. The verbal component will include questions about the alleged abuse, opportunities to discuss other people or relationships that may have caused similar distress, and a chance for the child to ask questions about the process, what will be done with the information gathered, or anything else that may be on the child's mind. Play techniques may include inviting a child to draw his or her family and talk about relationships between family members (if the alleged abuse was in the family), having a child draw pictures of the alleged abuse, or asking the child to act it out with play figures or in a dollhouse. At times anatomically detailed dolls may be used. These are cloth dolls with detailed male and female genitalia, breasts, openings for the mouth, anus and vagina, fingers and tongues, which can be used to show in detail who was touched where by whom and how. The interview progresses from the general to the specific. Whenever possible the interviewer will let the child take the lead, asking open-ended and nonspecific questions to avoid suggesting answers to the child. Once the general information is discussed, specific questions about the allegations at hand may be asked as well.

After information has been collected, the interviewer will spend a few minutes giving support to the child for doing a good job with difficult material and may offer some kind of food or toy reward for the effort made. Care is taken not to reward *what* was said, as this may suggest to the child that certain answers are more acceptable to the interviewer. This could lead a child to embroider the truth in order to please the adults. Instead, the *fact* of talking is praised; the bravery necessary to talk about hard things and the strength that it shows is emphasized.

The diagnostic interview and subsequent therapy when necessary can be very important sources of information to families. It can be very hard to know whether a child is telling the truth or lying, for instance, and families often need the assistance of a professional to sort out this issue. Children do lie, of course, though more often to get out of trouble ("No, I didn't break that cookie jar! There must have been a hungry thief") than to get into trouble. Telling about child sexual abuse is seldom rewarding for children and is not the sort of thing frequently lied about. Sometimes children may be coached, but a professional can typically spot the age-inappropriate language used or hear the "canned" quality of the accusations, which may not have the emotional or psychological reality of a real situation. Older children may be seeking revenge or trying to get someone in trouble with a false accusation, but again, the details of the accusation and the way in which it is told usually give the storyteller away. The whole issue of "false memory syndrome"—the concern that an accusation of sexual abuse may be suggested to a child in such a way that he or she believes it to be true when, in fact, nothing has occurred—is beyond the scope of this book. It is apparent to me, however, after interviewing more than a thousand sexually abused children, that the incidence of false report is far smaller than the rate of truthful allegations and that family and friends do better to believe the accusation initially and give the child the benefit of the doubt until all of the data is collected.

If the protective services worker has concerns about the psychological health of members of the family providing care for the child or who might have access as a visitor to the child, a *psychiatric evaluation* may be requested. This will involve one or more family members meeting with a psychiatrist, who will evaluate their ability to cope with all that has happened and function in a way that is safe and comfortable for themselves and the involved children. The psychiatrist will be trying to answer questions such as "Is the proposed custodian able to care for the children and keep them safe?" or "Is the alleged abuser stable enough to be allowed monitored visits with the children at this time?" Drug and alcohol histories will also be explored. The psychiatrist may offer medication or suggest further treatment to those involved.

After the results of these and possibly other evaluations are returned to the protective services worker, a service plan is developed in consultation with the family. If there is not sufficient evidence to believe that abuse took place (generally about 25 percent sure—a low level of proof), the case will be closed. Because no one can know for sure that abuse did not occur, only that it was not confirmed, cases are said to be "unsubstantiated" or "unfounded" when they are closed. If there is reason to believe that a child *was* abused, several options are available to the protective services department. A detailed service plan will be developed with input from the family and whatever professional evaluators have been involved to this point. This plan could include recommendations for therapy or medical treatment, changes in who has access to a child or to the place or where a child lives, and recommendations about what parents or other adults in a child's life need to do.

If the family is in agreement and cooperative with the plan, the case may be kept open for a brief period of time (usually six months to a year) to facilitate the provision of services in the community. A protective services worker will keep in monthly contact with the family during this period.

If the family is not cooperative with the plan or disputes the need to participate in services, the protective services agency may elect to take the family to family court (if they believe that the child is at risk if the plan is not followed), and a judge may order the family to follow the plan.

The Police Response

The police response runs parallel to the child protective services response. The investigations can be more or less coordinated depending upon the jurisdiction. In some areas only one interview is done with the child. Sometimes the police will do it, sometimes the social services agency, sometimes both together. One department may conduct the interview with the other behind a one-way mirror. Or one may videotape it and share the information with the other. In other areas each investigation proceeds on its own with two sets of interviews with the child and family.

However it is conducted, the purpose of the police investigation is to determine if a crime has been committed. Put simply, it is against the law to abuse children, and police investigate crimes. They will interview victims, witnesses and alleged perpetrators, collecting information that can be used as evidence if the case goes to trial. Parties involved have the right to a lawyer's presence when being questioned. The lawyers can object to questions and advise their clients when to answer and when to remain silent. The police gather evidence and coordinate with the district attorney to determine whether or not to file criminal charges against the alleged perpetrator and seek the legally specified penalties for child sexual abuse.

The ways in which the roles of the police and the child protective services departments differ can be confusing and infuriating to families. Child protective services may proceed as if a child is at risk and even consider a case substantiated (at the level of certainty that they require, around 25 percent sure) while the police are still doing preliminary investigations and have not yet interviewed any potential witnesses. Because the police need evidence that will stand up in court and point to a specific suspect as being guilty of a specified crime, families may already be in treatment and well on the way to putting the abuse behind them before the police even arrest a suspect. Their responsibilities require systematic investigation and careful collection of data, and they must not by hurrying lose the level of detail necessary to be sure that everyone's rights are protected. If the police investigation determines that there is credible evidence that a crime has been committed, the matter will move on to criminal court. There the district attorney will present the evidence collected by the police and seek to prove that a crime has been committed, asking for the appropriate penalties under the law.

Court Actions

Two distinct court systems are often involved in child sexual abuse situations.

In *family court* the question being considered is the safety of the child. The child protective service agency (and whatever branch of government is in charge in a particular jurisdiction) seeks to prove that a minor is at risk of abuse or that abuse has occurred and that a specific action or set of actions needs to take place to keep the child safe. The court may be requested to order a change in guardianship, to order monitored visits (visits with a responsible adult present to make sure nothing inappropriate happens to a child) or no visits with an alleged abuser, to order a child placed in a foster home, or to order that the family complete certain service requirements within a specified amount of time. If the family has refused to participate in the service plan developed by the child protective agency for the family members, the court proceeding may be seen as an adversarial proceeding. If the family is participating in the service plan, it may be seen as a supportive step to make sure services are made available or protection put in place for a child. For instance, the court may order a minor and his or her mother into therapy, provide protective service assistance for six months to help to get community services in place, and order the alleged abuser to get a psychological evaluation before he or she is allowed to see the child again. No determination is made of the innocence or guilt of the alleged abuser; only what is necessary for the safety of the child is considered. The burden of proof is lower—with a certainty of only 51 percent, the court may order protective steps taken.

In *criminal court*, on the other hand, the question is the guilt or innocence of an alleged abuser who has been accused of a specific crime or crimes against a specific child or children. The district attorney, in the name of the state, brings charges against the defendant and presents the evidence collected by the police in an effort to prove the defendant guilty. He or she is represented by a lawyer who seeks to establish innocence. The burden of proof is higher—"beyond a doubt" or about 95 percent sure that the crime took place and was committed by the defendant. Typically a criminal trial will have a jury unless the defendant waives it. If found guilty, the defendant will be given time in jail or a fine as punishment for the crime. In some cases he or she may also be liable to pay damages to the victims.

While the differences between the two courts are important—especially regarding their focus and the possible outcomes of their actions—the similarities are likely to be striking to participants not used to being a part of the judicial system. In both cases the proceedings are heard in a courtroom in front of a judge. The proceedings are adversarial—that is, there is a winner and a loser—and each side is trying to prove its case and triumph over the other. The specific procedures and ways of handling evidence vary from one court to another, but the need for legal representation to help a family through the frequently unfamiliar maze of legal language and procedures is the same for each.

The child alleging abuse and possibly other family members may be called upon to testify in either setting. The experience is similar in each court (though without the jury in the case of family court). A witness is called and sworn in, promising to tell the truth in what he or she is about to say with a "so help me God" and a hand on the Bible. After instructions by the judge, questions will be asked by attorneys for all those involved, one at a time, with each attorney being able to object to the questions asked before the witness answers if the attorney feels that the question is not appropriate according to the rules of that particular court. A witness should wait until the attorneys have had a chance to object and the judge rules on the matter before answering the question. The judge is the final arbitrator of whatever occurs in the courtroom. A witness who is confused or unsure how to proceed may always ask the judge for guidance. After all the attorneys have had a chance to ask their questions, the witness is dismissed by the judge and may leave the witness stand. In most cases witnesses are not allowed to listen to the rest of the case as it proceeds, though there is some variation on this.

Sometimes before actually going to the court to testify, witnesses are asked to give a sworn statement in the presence of attorneys for all concerned. This is called a deposition and has the same weight as a court appearance. Once this has been given, a witness may or may not actually need to go to court to testify.

The court system is not set up with children in mind. The technical language used and extended procedures are even more confusing and tiring for children than they are for adults. Most courts have waiting rooms for children, with age-appropriate furnishings and toys to help them manage stress and pass the time while awaiting their turn to testify. Before the day of their testimony, children may be offered a tour of the court and opportunity to sit in the witness chair and ask questions about what will actually happen once court begins. The judge will often meet with a child before he or she needs to come to court, in order to made the proceeding less scary, and will sometimes talk to the child in the judge's chamber to avoid the more frightening setting of the open courtroom.

Even with preparation by their lawyers and their therapists to tell the truth as they remember it and not be afraid of talking about such an intimate matter as sexual abuse in a room full of strangers, many children freeze in the courtroom and are not able to give "credible testimony." If the police or district attorney can predict ahead of time that, due to the child's age, the nature of the trauma suffered, threats made by the alleged abuser, or some other reason, the child is not likely to be able to give testimony that will meet the standards necessary in the court, a decision may be made not to have the child testify—even if that means that there will be no case against the alleged abuser. It can be very difficult to decide which is best for a child: to avoid retraumatizing him or her by a court appearance, or to seek justice in the court (a step that may have its own rewards for a child as well as for society at large). A family may need help in understanding why a specific decision was made in their case.

Because the two courts function autonomously, it is possible to have proceedings going forward in each of the settings independently. Sometimes the transcripts of the one proceeding will be made available to the other, but because the focus and the rules are different in each setting, this is often not done. Things can become very confusing for families when the outcomes of the two courts differ. If a grandfather, for instance, was ordered by family court to have no contact with his granddaughter, who alleged that he sexually abused her, but he maintained his innocence despite physical evidence that the girl was molested and despite her story that he did it—and then he was found innocent by the criminal court with its higher standard of evidence, what is the family to believe about whether or not he did in fact molest her? The apparent contradiction may never be resolved.

Other Aspects of the System Response
Other players may be called in to help in a specific family's situation beyond the cast of characters. If bite marks or damage to the mouth or teeth is a part of the evidence against the alleged abuse, a forensic dentist might become involved. If in-home assistance is needed with parenting issues or child management, a parent aide may be assigned to the family. Other specialists (translators, mobility aides and so on) will also be assigned as needed.

Some areas have a coordinating committee that seeks to make sure communication flows between the systems involved and that the needs of the child and family are not lost in the midst of the demand of courts and the investigators involved. The family may not even ever meet these people, though in some instances they may make their services available to the family directly. Families will, however, be asked to sign consent forms for the release of information to these groups, and they will have a right to know who is involved in discussing their situation.

Exiting the System

It may seem to a family that the "help"—sometimes unwanted—provided by the various components of the system will never end, but each component does actually have review dates and exit procedures in place from the very beginning of interaction with a family. When a child is considered no longer at risk for abuse or has satisfactorily begun the process of healing and is connected with appropriate professionals, the child protective services staff will close the case. Once a family has met the requirements imposed by the family court (which are monitored by the child protective services), the court will bow out of their lives. Most jurisdictions have a time limit for how long families can stay in the system if the adults show no interest in or ability to meet the requirements of the court. A two-year period before parental rights are terminated is typical. The actions of the criminal court can be appealed by the defendant found guilty, but this too eventually ends.

In the midst of all that is going on, it is easy to feel that all of these appointments and deliberations will go on forever. One of the most important encouragements that can be given to a family in the midst of the system response to alleged child sexual abuse is that it *will* all end, and life *will* be resumed again with some semblance of normalcy.

Armed with a better understanding of the systems that families will need to deal with after an allegation of child sexual abuse is made, the person seeking to be of help is in a better position to know how to be of assistance each step along the way. The next chapter addresses how the church can be of help.

4

How Can the Church Help?

Helping Children & Families
While Caring for Caregivers

"Of course we'd be glad to keep praying for you and your family. Don't think twice about calling us anytime day or night, John. What's happening today?"

"We just thought we'd get somewhere in court, that's all. Suzie was all prepped to testify against my brother about what he did to her—she toured the courtroom yesterday. (And Chris, thank Laura again for going downtown with Jackie and Suzie yesterday. I don't think Jackie could have faced it alone, and I can't take more time off from work.) The lawyer and Dr. George had prepared her for what to expect, and Suzie had her teddy with her for safety. Then to get it all continued because the lawyer for the bum of a brother of mine was sick! How much can a six-year-old take?"

"Or her family. Listen, we're headed over to the church at 7:30 for the kids' programs. You guys want to come over for dinner first and just decompress? There's plenty. Then maybe we could drop the kids off at the church for their

classes and the four of us could find a quiet place to talk and pray."
"Sounds great. Let me check with Jackie."

While that dialogue sounds pretty ordinary, most families I know who have been through sexual abuse and the aftermath in the legal system would have loved to have brothers and sisters in Christ who were available, compassionate, understanding, and still treated them and their families like normal people. In this vignette John needed to talk about his frustration with the court process, his anger at his brother (the alleged perpetrator), and his concern for his wife and daughter. Chris reminded him of his availability at any hour, listened without judging or giving pat solutions, offered practical and spiritual support, and made concrete his availability to help. This chapter will look at what families need as their reaction to child sexual abuse unfolds, and how the pastoral staff and others in their church can respond in a way that lives out the biblical mandate to "bear one another's burdens and so fulfill the law of Christ." Several areas of concern that frequently impact children, their families and those who seek to help them will be discussed in turn.

Isolation
Perhaps the hardest thing to keep in mind is that children who have been sexually abused must not be defined solely by that experience. All too often parents feel sorry for their children and perhaps guilty for not being able to protect them better. They begin to overcompensate for what happened to their children: they don't require them to do chores, feed them only their favorite foods, no longer punish them for misbehavior. The result can be a child who is resented by his or her siblings for receiving special treatment and rejected by peers for being selfish and demanding. Parents must keep up the usual way of treating their children, while adding whatever special attention is needed to help the abused child. Friends and those who seek to minister to these children and their families should do the same.

This advice may seem strange to those who have not walked a family through dealing with child sexual abuse. Yet, surprisingly, for many families who have dealt with molestation a major complaint is the isolation they feel from their friends and church community. Some people pull back out of fear, not knowing if they might somehow say the "wrong" thing. Others do not like the feelings that arise within themselves when confronted with the real presence of evil in the world that child sexual abuse represents. Discovering that a friend's daughter has been molested can make people uncomfortable about the safety of their own children. One way to deal with this discomfort is to avoid contact with those who bring the uncomfortable things to mind. Friends may also assume that a family wishes to be alone— but while this may be true for some, for many the opposite is the case. The best way to find out is to ask. You might say, "I know this is a hard time for you and your family. Would you like to spend some time together to take your mind off of it or would you rather be alone? We just want to help but don't know how." Your question offers assistance without adding to the demands on the family by insisting that they accept. It acknowledges wishing to help despite not knowing how to do so.

A move toward isolation can come from the side of the abused child and his or her family as well. Children may see themselves as damaged or different. Many believe that they somehow look different because of the abuse or that they are now bad or tainted. The child who raises this concern verbally should be reassured that he or she is still cared for and precious to family, friends and God. Others never say a word about how different they are feeling but begin to isolate themselves from peers because they feel they are different or even poisonous to their friends. To reach the many children who carry this fear but do not raise it explicitly, children who have been molested should still be included in activities, invited to sleepovers and treated as they would have been treated if the abuse were still a secret. (The major exception is those abuse-reactive children who, because of their behavior in response to having been abused, may present a risk to others. Such a case requires a response that targets the elimination of the unacceptable behavior to keep a child and others safe and yet supports the child as he or she seeks to overcome the abuse.)

The resources available in Christ may be of special value in these situations. The power of the Holy Spirit working in a child or family through the prayer of fellow believers must not be underestimated. Paul, in Ephesians 3:20-21, reminds us of "him who is able to do immeasurably more than all we ask or imagine, according to his power that is at work within us." Those dealing with the pain and trauma of child sexual abuse may forget the resources they have in Christ, and others can lift them up in prayer. Reminders of the truth of who God is and who we are in relationship to him, as revealed in Scripture, may be of great help. The reminder in Romans 8 that nothing can separate us from the love of God and the truth that "in all things we are more than conquerors" may not be emotionally real to those in the midst of dealing with a child who has been abused, but the gentle reminder of these truths, the practical outworkings of which may not yet be evident, will be reassuring to many. If, after you offer these truths to children or families, they still do not feel better, gently remind them that their feelings are still wounded from the trauma that they have been through and encourage them to believe that the truth of God as revealed in Scripture is accurate, even when they do not feel that it is. Do not enter into prolonged arguments—that is the last thing they need! Rather, lovingly listen to their pain. If they feel discouraged or tell you that the depth to which they feel hurt shows that they are not good Christians, remind them that they have a good reason for feeling so bad, that it is normal to feel the way they do. Then when you are alone, pray for them as they are unable to pray for themselves.

If you are part of a sacramental tradition, use that resource as well. Confession and Eucharist have a powerful psychological cleansing and restoration effect on people as well as a spiritual import. One six-year-old boy felt that his uncle's abuse had made him bad—that somehow by participating in the abuse he had not only done something evil but become evil. The family belonged to a church tradition that emphasized confession and communion. With the help of their parish priest, the boy was reassured of God's forgiveness and love for him in the spiritual tradition with which his family and he were most comfortable.

Families, too, isolate themselves out of shame and embarrassment (especially if the alleged perpetrator is a family member) or to spare friends the difficulty of dealing with their own discomfort about the abuse.

This can happen at the time when they most need fellowship and support, and their church needs to reach out to them and enfold them back into the community. Their increased sensitivity at this time may lead to the perception of slights even when none was intended, so extra care must be taken to be certain they know that they are welcome. They may feel that everyone in the church has labeled them and is gossiping about them behind their backs. They must be reassured that this is not so. If it *is* so, then another problem exists that church leadership needs to address with the body.

Labeling and Gossip

Two issues that go hand in hand are labeling and gossip. It is hard to gossip about a real person about whom you care, for whom you are praying, and with whom you are interacting regularly. If, however, that person can be reduced to a label or example of a particular category, it becomes easier to categorize, generalize and dismiss that person. This is a danger in a child sexual abuse scenario where one could easily assign roles such as "victim," "villains," "uncaring parent" and so on and go to town on the reputations of the people in each of those roles, forgetting that real people, all of whom have strengths and weaknesses, and all of whom are loved by God, fill each role.

The damage done to children and their families when rumors are believed and gossip spread is incalculable. Child sexual abuse often leads to feelings of betrayal and the awareness that people who had previously been trusted are, in fact, untrustworthy. The Christian community must not repeat this damage at a time when abused children and their families are depending on their community for help and support. Scripture is clear on the damage that can be caused by the tongue. The stakes are high: not only the additional pain caused to people already suffering, or the damage it does to the person who spreads the gossip, but the relationship with God of those damaged by his people. I have seen many who have walked away from God and the church when people have failed them in this way.

This tragedy is best prevented by careful attention to gossip and rumors before an abusive incident occurs. If members of the church have been helped to mature in the control of their tongues prior to an abusive event, it is more likely that they will behave appropriately when challenged. Once the abuse occurs and is becoming known in the community, a decision should be made about how to proceed in consultation with the family. The minister might make an announcement from the pulpit that the Smith family would appreciate prayer and support as they go through a difficult time. There is no need to share the details of the difficulty facing the family—in general, the less said publicly the better. Depending upon the size and structure of the church, however, some families find it helpful to appoint a spokesperson who will share information, needs and prayer requests with the congregation. Even without knowing all the data, however, the church should put into action whatever supports it offers to members in times of crisis. Whoever organizes meals and other ministry to families in distress could mobilize that resource. Babysitters, emergency loans when needed, counseling and prayer support should be offered as necessary.

Another challenge to church leadership and those in ministry to sexually abused children and their families is to avoid sliding into dealing with stereotypes rather than real people. It is all too easy to minister to what ought to be there or what the experts say a child of a certain age should be feeling rather than to take the time to ask the questions, listen to the answers and get to know the specific child and family in front of you. It can be difficult to predict the degree of trauma that an experience will generate for a child, for instance. The commonsense expectation is that the more severe the molestation or the worse the incident of child sexual abuse, the worse the child's symptoms and trauma will be. But in reality much of the damage done depends on the vulnerability of the child and the support systems available. I have seen children where long-time sexual abuse within the family was not as devastating as a one-time encounter with a stranger. Be certain to assess the impact on each family member in each situation, and do not be too quick to think that you know what must be happening.

Loyalties
Another issue a church community needs to consider is whom to trust and whom to side with when both the alleged victim and the alleged abuser are

a part of the same congregation. While there may be a desire to minister to and support both sides, this is usually not possible unless the family is part of a large congregation with multiple services and a large ministerial staff. In that case it may be possible, for example, to set up a situation where the victim goes to the first service and is ministered to and supported by the youth pastor, and the alleged abuser goes to the second service and is cared for by the young-adult pastor. Even then the complications of how to manage who gets to go on the church picnic or attend the talk by the visiting missionary are difficult to manage, and conflicts between church members who support one side or the other are inevitable. It is generally preferable for either the victim or the alleged abuser to attend a different church, at least while the investigation is conducted. This may in fact become a necessity if, for instance, a restraining order is in place, mandating that the alleged abuser not come within 1,000 feet of the victim. In such cases, encouraging the child and his or her family to attend the same worship service as the alleged abuser may result in the child's being removed and placed in a foster home because the parents were in violation of the court order and were judged not to be protecting the child.

When conflicting loyalties arise, parties supporting both sides must be reminded that they are not the ones conducting the investigation and that it is not their place to judge or condemn either side of the conflict. Each side is likely to be unhappy with some part of the investigation process and to share their frustration (and appropriately so) with those who are supporting them through the ordeal. When the supporters of each side compare notes, conflict may arise. For the sake of the congregation, these feuds should be identified and the participants reminded to exercise charity toward one another.

Symptoms

Sexual abuse is often first brought to the attention of the adults in a child's world by the symptoms that the child shows. Discussed in detail earlier, these symptoms can be difficult to deal with and often present a challenge for families of abused children and those dealing with them as they seek to be of help to the molested children.

There is often a great deal of discomfort with some of the things that abused children may do or say. Some may need to work through their abusive experience by talking about it, and they do not always choose the same situations to talk in that the adults in their world might want them to choose. Sometimes the material comes up spontaneously in the child's talk or play. He or she may be playing quietly with a friend and suddenly confide that his Uncle Tommy has a large penis and sometimes asks him or her to play with it. Parents or other adults in charge can remind children in these situations that this is not something to be talked about with everyone but only with their parents and special people like doctors or others with whom their parents tell them to talk to about it. Other children seek to work through their abusive experience by replicating it with dolls or other toys. These children may show sexually explicit scenes with Barbie and Ken or draw human figures engaged in sexual activities or with large genitalia. In a calm voice, adults in the setting where this occurs should redirect them to another activity without drawing the attention of any other children who might be in the area to the sexualized play, then talk to them privately about what they were thinking or feeling that led to this game. Most children can learn when it is and is not appropriate to draw, play or talk about their abusive experience. Those who have trouble internalizing the limits may need to talk to a professional who can help them come to terms with their concerns and learn to discuss them only in the appointed places.

When children's sexualized activities are directed toward adults, they may place themselves at risk of being reabused if the adult to whom they direct the activities does not have appropriate boundaries. When a five-year-old rubs the inside of an adult's leg and asks "Do you like it when I touch you there?" adults need to know that this is not provocative behavior but a replication of abusive interactions and may in fact be meant as a compliment by the child, who intends to be affectionate and intimate. This behavior must not be ignored or responded to with disgust, but rather dealt with directly and clearly. Telling the child "I like it when you touch me, but that is not a good place for a child to be touching a grown man [or woman]" sets a limit and reassures the child that he or she is still cared for. Further direction such as "Why don't you put your arm around my shoulder instead?" can offer a positive way to express physical affection.

A more difficult problem arises when a child seeks mastery through repetition of the sexual abuse with other children. This most often happens with the child playing the role of the actor rather than acted upon, doing to others what was done to him or her. Although aware that their sexualized behavior is not proper, and often despite their desire to stop repeating the abuse that they suffered with others, these children may be unable to stop aggressing sexually on others. They should be separated from the children with whom they are playing the sexual games and brought to a professional skilled in dealing with these issues. The mental health worker will seek to understand the particular motivation that leads to their assaultive behavior and the patterns of their actions, in order to help their families plan interventions to bring the offenses to a stop. A child who is confusing intimacy and sexuality, seeking to express caring in the wrong ways (as in the example earlier in this chapter), needs different assistance than one who is still angry over how he or she was hurt and is seeking to hurt others to reduce his or her own pain. A skilled therapist will know how to differentiate these and other situations that might lead to the behavior and how to help a child and family develop new patterns.

Response of Others

A common issue for families seeking to deal with the intrusion of child sexual abuse into their lives is not knowing how to handle the response of other people. Sometimes this takes the form of wondering whom they should tell and how much they should say. When the abuse has become public knowledge (or at least known within the church community or family circle), the issue is how to deal with the fact that people already know intimate facts concerning a family and with changes (or perceived changes) in the way they treat the family.

When the question of whom to tell is still under the family's control, the best advice is generally to tell as few people as necessary. Knowledge of the fact of the abuse will almost always change the way a child is thought of and treated, and it may impact the relationships of other family members as well. Some professionals may need to know details of what happened—

a child's primary health care provider, for instance, or a therapist treating the child or other family members. Family members may feel that it is helpful to tell others close to them—a minister, close friend or member of the extended family, for example. Before they do, however, they should consider whether or not that person has proven to be trustworthy in the past and consider what harm might be done if whatever they tell that person were to be passed on to others.

As children become older and more aware of the impact their abuse has on others, they may have opinions about who should or should not be told. Their opinions should be considered but need not always rule the actions of adults in the family. A child may not want his or her grandparents to know about abuse out of fear that they would love them less, but parents who know the grandparents better may want to overrule the child's objections so that the child discovers what the parents already know—that nothing could diminish a grandma's and grandpa's love. (Of course, in situations where the child is right, and his or her assessment of a friend or family member is shared by the parents, no information needs to be given.) Conversely, a child may be indiscriminate in sharing information or want to tell a friend or family member whom the parents or guardians feel would not be able to handle the information. In this case, their reason for feeling that way should be shared with the child. Ultimately the child will make the decision whether or not to talk about his or her own experiences, and adults need to be prepared to accept that reality. Forbidding children to talk, or reacting with anger when it becomes apparent that they have done so, is counterproductive and creates more tension and division at a time when the family needs to be working together.

Once the information is public, a family needs to be careful to distinguish between how their extended family and friends are actually reacting and how the family may be misperceiving the reactions based on their own expectations and fears. People may pull back simply because they do not know what to say, but their withdrawal may be seen by the family as confirmation of their fear that no one likes them anymore or as a sign of God's displeasure and rejection as mediated by his church. Clarity of communication becomes important here. Families under the stress of dealing with child sexual abuse are seldom in the best frame of mind to have difficult conversations with friends and family members to clarify what they might be thinking or feeling that has led to the behavioral changes. Extended family and friends need to deal with their emotions and reactions on their own time and not impose them on the abuse victim's family, seeking instead to be supportive and minister the love of Christ into that family's pain.

Shame and Guilt

Early on, for the family of a child sexual abuse victim and for the child, the issues of shame and guilt will emerge. They may remain during and after the investigation and court proceedings. *Shame* refers to a sense of having done something or been a party to something that makes us feel less than we think we should be. An internal judgment is made, and we find ourselves wanting. Shame has to do with who a person *is*.

Guilt refers to having made a mistake and objectively being guilty as measured against an external standard. We feel we have failed to meet a standard—our own or someone else's—and we feel bad or unworthy or ineligible for the good things in life. Guilt has to do with things a person has *done*. Shame and guilt go hand in hand for many.

Children may feel different from their peers as a result of the shame that they feel over having been abused. Because, for many, their internal reality has been shattered by the impact of the betrayal or guilt they experienced, they may believe that they look different on the outside and that everyone who looks at them knows about the abuse. Reassurances that they look nice, are fun to be with, and liked by peers and adults help to address this concern. If a child insists that he or she is bad or deserves to be punished, seek to find out why before jumping in with reassurances. The child may have an irrational thought that he or she needs help facing and correcting. (For instance, something like "I don't just *do* bad things. Now that Uncle Tommy touched me, I was turned into bad and even the good I do is bad too," as a six-year-old once said to me.) Or they may have a realistic concern that can be addressed and resolved (such as feeling bad that they have not told the whole story of what happened to them in their abusive experiences or worried that people are mad at them for not getting better quicker). In either case their concerns should be listened to supportively, then addressed in the light of reality.

Families and others involved with child sexual abuse struggle with guilt and shame too. It is important to help them differentiate between true guilt and false guilt. True guilt is based upon actions knowingly taken that resulted in harm to others. If a church board knew that a candidate for pastor had a history of sexual abuse allegations against him from other churches and called him anyway without seeking to clarify the situation, and he fell into sexual sin again, then they would have an objective and real reason to be guilty. They would be suffering from true guilt and should follow biblical mandates—confession of sin to God and possibly to those wronged (except where it would cause further harm), asking for forgiveness from God and possibly those wronged, and seeking to make restitution as best as they are able. False guilt is a reaction to the horror of the situation and is often tied to a wish that things had been different along with a belief that one should have done something to make them so. A parent who has done everything that he or she should have done since the abuse allegations came to light but keeps berating himself or herself with statements such as "I should have known what was going on" or "A good parent would have spotted it and stopped it" is likely laboring under false guilt. The parent needs to look at the facts and come to an understanding that there was nothing that he or she could have done differently given the known facts at the time. This process may take some time. Professional help may be required, especially when the need to maintain one's guilt serves as a defense against even more intolerable feelings about the apparent randomness of the universe or anger against God for allowing such evil to happen.

Paul's teaching in Romans 8 that all have sinned and fallen short of the glory of God can help those who are feeling uniquely sinful and unforgivable for either real or false guilt. Despite the differentiation made and the labels applied to the two types of guilt to highlight the different sorts of interventions needed, both feel real to those who suffer from them, and the comfort of Scripture verses that address these issues cannot be overemphasized. Those who believe that there is no hope for them to be forgiven can often find reassurance in the story of the prodigal son recounted in Luke 15 and the fact that the father sought out his child while the child was still far off. The distinction that the son's guilt was the result of his own choice, whereas the victim's or family's guilt is the result of the actions of others, does not seem to matter to people feeling separated from God. They may find comfort in the fact that even in the case of objective guilt (unlike their own) God is able to forgive. The reality that Christ came into the world to save sinners (1 Tim 1:15) can often remind people that the separation from God they feel is due to their own issues, not to God's having changed his opinion of them. God's loving initiatives toward humanity can bring relief from both guilt and shame, and counseling and prayer ministries that use these truths as a foundation can have a profound impact on abuse victims and their families.

These and other issues can often be dealt with constructively in the context of the Christian community. At other times the depth of the damage done by child sexual abuse requires professional therapeutic interventions for children, their families or both. Chapter five considers the question of therapy for child sexual abuse.

5

What About Therapy?

Choosing the Right Course

"And then the social worker from the child protective agency told me that I needed to send Kevin to therapy. Therapy! Can you believe that, Pastor Carol? Like he's crazy or something. But I knew you'd back me up, so I told her I didn't need her ungodly therapists to heal Kevin. Jesus is enough. Isn't that right, pastor?"

"Jesus certainly is the source of our healing, but I wonder if we should be limiting God's tools to those we choose, Karen. After all, when you broke your leg skiing last winter, you asked for prayer—and you also saw a doctor to have it set."

"But that's different. Medical doctors are one thing, but to have someone messing with my Kevin's mind—he's only eight. And you know that psychology is not Christian. Besides, how would I find anyone good?"

"You're assuming a lot of negatives, Karen. It's precisely because he is only eight that Kevin needs someone to help him sort out what happened with his

uncle. The therapist may be a believer—and even if not, a good therapist will respect your beliefs and work within them. There are a few people in our church who have been in therapy—let me call around today and see if any of them saw someone who is good with kids and knowledgeable about sexual abuse issues. Will you be at home later so I can get back to you?"

This vignette may seem too full of issues in just a few sentences to be realistic, but all of these concerns—and more—race though parents' heads when someone suggests or orders therapy for their child. People may dislike being told what to do by a child protective worker, or they may resent the suggestion that their child needs help beyond what they as the parents can give. Christian families are often suspicious of therapists and psychology, fearing ungodly methods or goals. Families unfamiliar with the mental health world may feel overwhelmed or discouraged about what type of help they need or how to find a good therapist.

This chapter begins by considering how to know if a child or family member needs behavioral health treatment to help with his or her response to child sexual abuse. A brief overview of the types of therapists available is followed by advice on how to pick one. We will discuss what to expect, both in terms of procedures and issues covered, as well as how to know when it is time to stop.

When Is Therapy Needed?

Simply put, therapy, like medical treatment, is needed when something is wrong—if a child or family member is having worries or problems, or if something is not going as well with the family as its members might have hoped. "If it isn't broken, don't fix it" works as a motto for behavioral health interventions as well as in many other spheres of family life. Knowing what is broken or might break is more complicated here than in many other areas. The following are some tips on what might indicate a need for therapy, first for the child, then for family members.

Indications That a Child Needs Professional Help

Many of the symptoms discussed in chapter one as indicative of child sexual abuse will diminish or even disappear once the abuse has been brought to light and stopped. With the implementation of the suggestions of the last chapter, even more issues will be resolved and even more problematic behaviors should disappear. When they do not—when they continue or increase—professional help should be considered to determine why a child cannot get back on track and to see what interventions are needed to help him or her do so. Of particular concern are the following:

Sleep disturbances. Nightmares, difficulty getting to sleep, awakening in the middle of the night and thinking about what happened, climbing into an adult's bed because it feels safer, and sleeping much more than prior to the abusive experience are all examples of sleep disturbances that may be secondary to child sexual abuse. They may be indicative of anxiety, posttraumatic stress disorder or depression.

Fears, phobias and avoidant behaviors. Children who have been abused may become overly frightened. Sometimes these fears are related specifically to the abusive experience, such as a fear of going to sleep-away camp again, if that is where the abuse occurred. Other times the fears generalize to the point where the child is afraid to be away from familiar places or people that the child considers safe to the extent that he or she will not go to school or be away from the presence of his or her mother. When these fears are long-lived and interfere with living a normal life, then professional help should be sought.

Sexualized play or sexual acting out with adults. Whether in solitary activities or with peers, sexualized play after child sexual abuse is a warning sign that needs attention. Children may be seeking mastery of their trauma through repetition of what happened to them, either playing the same role of victim or taking on the role of aggressor. After they have been told not to do so, and if age-appropriate explanations and discipline have not worked to help them to stop this behavior, professional help should be called in. Similarly, if interactions with adults are becoming sexualized due to actions on the child's part (for instance, a child is wanting to sit next to and touch the youth group leader in a way that is uncomfortable for the leader and inappropriate to the relationship), and if this behavior does not stop even after attempts to redirect and counsel the child, professional help is needed.

Repeated discussion of the abuse or refusal to discuss the abuse at all. Children who cannot stop talking about their abusive experience to one and all, even after seeing the responses of others and being told how negatively this affects the way people see them, have not been able to work through their feelings about what has happened to them. They need to be directed to talk about it with someone who has been trained to help them come to resolution. Similarly, children showing distress in symptoms only, not talking but rather withdrawing from everyone, need to be taken to see someone who can help to draw them out, enabling them to talk about what needs to be talked about.

A request for help by the child. At times a child may know that he or she is in trouble and ask for the opportunity to talk with a therapist. This often happens when children have had previous experience with a counselor that they found helpful. They may also have heard about therapy from friends or in the media. Parents may respond by feeling that their child should just come to them—that there is no need for an outsider to get involved. Their feelings may be hurt, or they may minimize the difficulties that their child is having. This is a disservice to a child who recognizes the need for help and trusts the parents enough to go to them for assistance. It is often easier for a child to talk to someone outside of the family situation, someone who is not involved and whose feelings do not need to be protected from what may be said. Even if the symptoms do not seem extreme to them, wise parents will see the call for help for what it is and seek the aid that their child needs, rather than waiting for the situation to deteriorate further.

Encouragement to seek help by professionals or those who know the child well. This message can also be difficult for parents to hear. School counselors, youth ministers and child protective services workers have the advantage of being outside of the family looking in, and they have experience working with others in similar situations to guide them as they suggest that there may be a need for help. These suggestions do not always come in the kindest and gentlest ways and may feel to parents like an accusation of failure or a challenge to their parental authority. It is necessary to look beyond the emotional response and ask what is really being said about the needs of the child. No harm is done by having an evaluation and listening to what a trained professional may say about the need for treatment.

In addition to the specific areas of concern listed above, parents should listen to their own intuition about their children. They are the ones who know their own kids best, and if they feel that an issue has been exacerbated by the abuse that their child suffered, then they ought to seek out help. An area that was already a problem for a child may be made worse by child sexual abuse. If a child had a tendency toward depression, abuse may push him or her further in that direction. A child who already withdrew into daydreams and fantasy to escape the pressures of life may, after an abusive experience, be so unfocused in the classroom that teachers are reporting that he or she is inattentive most of the time and is about to fail school. Like earthquakes that occur along fault lines where there was already a weakness in the earth's crust, the psychological problems that erupt after child sexual abuse often occur in areas that are already known to be areas of weakness for a child. Even if the cause does not seem to be directly attributable to the abusive experiences, help should be sought and the therapist told about the abuse so that he or she can correctly evaluate what is going on with a child and family.

Indications That a Family Member Needs Professional Help

Children are not the only ones to suffer in families when child sexual abuse has occurred, nor are they the only ones to need therapy to deal with the trauma. Several warning signs that might indicate the need for treatment for family members of abused children are discussed below.

Fascination with discussing the matter and refusing to let the child move on. The adult family members of a family in which child sexual abuse has occurred have a difficult balancing act that they must maintain in relationship to the victim. On the one hand, they must be available to the child if he or she decides to talk further about the abuse, seeking to help the child process whatever aspect of the experience is causing pain or distress at any given time. At the same time, they must be able to let go of the abuse when the child is not focused on it, refusing to define the child only by what happened in this area of his or her life. When adults keep pestering the child to talk about the abuse—to provide more information or tell the story just one more time—they are demonstrating that they need a place to talk about it and work it through at their own speed and for their own purposes. They must leave the child out of these conversations and pursue their own healing without making the child responsible for helping them to process what happened and how they are feeling about it. This is why they should seek professional help and leave the child free to work out the issues at his or her own pace. Often an inability to let go of these matters is a sign of guilt over what happened, an indication of unresolved feelings toward God for permitting it to occur, or a sign of their own sexual abuse history clouding their judgment in the present.

Overprotective reaction. The world can be a very dangerous place for children, and nothing brings this home to parents like having one of their children get hurt. Child sexual abuse in particular can lead parents to become more cautious about their children's whereabouts, their activities, their friends and their friends' families. This is not necessarily problematic in and of itself, but if parents' reactions become extreme to the point where they do not allow children age-appropriate freedoms, or if the parents themselves become unable to separate from the child without overwhelming worry or anxiety, they need a place to talk about their fears and help in developing a way to manage them. And this must be done without making the child, who has already been abused and may already be thinking of himself or herself as different even before a parent starts acting strange, pay too high a price for a parent's comfort. The parent (or other family member, since parents are not the only ones so affected) should seek counseling.

Distancing reaction. Sometimes one or more members of a family see the child who has been abused as "damaged goods" and tend to back away from him or her, favoring other children in the family. Such distancing can confirm the child's worst fears about himself or herself, and it can create a poor relationship between a child and other members of the family at a time when the child needs them most. Parents and other adults may also back away out of fear that they might be accused of inappropriate actions with a child or because the child's abuse reminds them of unresolved

aspects of their own. These may be red flags—signs of the need for help.
Reawakening of an adult's issues with his or her own childhood abusive experiences. At times, when a child is sexually abused, a parent or other family member is reminded of traumatic events from childhood—even previously unremembered events. This can throw an adult into turmoil and leave him or her not only unable to respond to the child in a helpful way but unable to continue managing his or her own life successfully. When this happens, professional assistance from someone outside of the family is helpful.

Activation of other personal or family issues in response to the stress of dealing with child sexual abuse. As mentioned earlier in reference to the impact child sexual abuse can have on a child, the impact of child sexual abuse on other adult family members can be like an earthquake that shakes loose all aspects of a person's life and causes ruptures in those areas already stressed and strained. In the aftermath of child sexual abuse, those who have a substance-abuse history may begin to drink or use drugs again, even after extensive periods of sobriety. Someone who has struggled with depression, anxiety attacks or some other psychiatric illness may be pushed back over the edge by the stresses of dealing with the abuse. Adults experiencing these setbacks should seek help both for their own good and so they can be more available to the child.

Looking for a Therapist

Assuming that for the reasons listed above, or for other good cause, you are looking for a therapist for your child or yourself, how can you find someone who will be of help? First, pray. God can lead you to the right person, often through unexpected means. Getting a recommendation from someone who knows you and knows the therapist is one of the best ways to make a connection. Presumably that person would have some reason for thinking that the two of you would make a good team, and, depending how well they in fact do know you, someone who has had a good experience with a therapist may be the best referral source. Another good resource is a minister, teacher, medical doctor or other professional whose work has brought him or her into contact with mental health care providers. Referral lists from trusted sources are also good—several Christian organizations (such as Focus on the Family, the Billy Graham Evangelistic Association, denominational bodies and others) have lists of licensed professional counselors who meet their standards for training and experience. If you are seeking to use health insurance to pay for a part of the cost of treatment, then you may need to choose from a list of providers covered under your insurance plan. The phone book is a last resource to find the names of mental health counselors in your area.

Once names are at hand, it is necessary to sort out which person or persons might be worth meeting with to consider as a therapist. Generally it is better to pick a licensed professional rather than someone unlicensed, because you can be certain a basic set of standards has been met. Which credentials are licensed varies from state to state, but in general the following categories of professionals are available to pick from:

Psychiatrists are medical doctors with specialized training in the use of psychotropic medications and, to one extent or another, training and experience in doing therapy. Psychiatrists have completed medical school and specialized training in brain biochemistry and mind/body relationships. They are licensed by the state in which they practice and cannot call themselves by this title unless they meet the state licensing criteria. These days many work in conjunction with other mental health professionals, providing medical backup and medication management for clients receiving treatment from other professionals when there is need of pharmacological treatment. Courts may order psychiatric assessment; then only a psychiatrist will do. Other times a mental health care provider from another related discipline may be a better and less expensive choice for assessment or ongoing treatment.

Psychologists are doctoral-level mental health practitioners who have completed four or more years of training beyond the B.A. level and completed both course work and intensive practical training in mental health. Some may have the traditional Ph.D. degree (Doctor of Philosophy in Psychology) while others have the Psy.D. (Doctor of Psychology) or another set of initials after their name. These different degrees represent differences in focus at the graduate schools where the clinicians studied. They are not as important in choosing a behavioral health care provider as experience with the problem that is bringing a family to treatment or with the specific age group of the child needing help. Whatever the degree, a licensed psychologist has a specified number of hours of supervised experience and has passed both national and state exams. In most areas it is illegal to call yourself a psychologist unless you are licensed. Some psychologists specialize in children or families; other are more general in their practice. A family should feel free to ask questions to get the information they need in order to feel confident of the person they choose.

Marriage and family therapists are counselors with a two-year post-B.A. degree in most cases; some have earned a Ph.D. in marriage and family therapy. In many but not all states this is a licensed or credentialed degree, and those who practice with this title must accumulate a specified number of supervised hours of experience and pass state and national tests to do so. As the name implies, these practitioners specialize in marriage and family issues; they may or may not have special expertise in child sexual abuse, depending on where they went to school and did practical training.

Social workers also have a two-year post-B.A. degree, focusing on training in therapy, systems analysis and case management, depending on the school and classes taken. Licensed (or credentialed, depending on the location) workers pass a state test and accumulate a specified number of supervised hours of experience before they may practice.

Other specialties may also be available: a *pastoral counselor,* someone trained in advising from a religious perspective, often an ordained person; a *nationally certified counselor,* a relatively new credential made available to those with two years of training beyond the B.A. who meet certain training and experience requirements; a *"Christian counselor,"* largely undefined except by the person using the title.

When licensed and credentialed, providers are generally accepted by most insurance companies for reimbursement. The fact that a provider is licensed assures the consumer of at least a certain level of competence and provides some accountability. Should something nonprofessional occur, a complaint could be filed with the state licensing authority and an investigation would follow. Many insurance companies also have their own credentials process for therapists who meet their criteria (and who, not incidentally, are willing to accept the payment per session that they offer). You should check to see whether and to what degree the therapist you are interested in seeing is covered by your insurance. Some companies will pay 80 percent of an "in-network" therapist's fee (that is, a therapist whom they have already credentialed and who has agreed to accept their preset payment as a fee) leaving you a copay of 20 percent of the fee. Some insurance companies may pay only 50 percent of an "out-of-network" therapist's fee (that is a licensed, credentialed provider not already approved by the company and who has not agreed to accept their fee). Other companies pay a different percentage of the fee depending upon what the diagnosis is. In some states the law requires parity between medical coverage and behavioral health coverage—that is, insurance companies must pay the same percentage of a behavioral health care provider's fee as they do a medical provider's fee—while in other states the percentage paid for each category varies greatly. The numbers used here are only examples and should be checked out on a case-by-case basis. If insurance reimbursement is not a factor, then a family may feel freer to pick an unlicensed person, especially if that provider has other characteristics that are especially important to the family (such as belonging to a particular denomination or offering a particular type of intervention).

Expertise in the area of child sexual abuse is probably the most important factor to look for in choosing a therapist for yourself or your child. No particular degree or school will guarantee that a practitioner has that experience. You will need to ask. Therapists are not offended by clients' questions about how many sexually abused children they have worked with. They understand that the clients are seeking to find someone who can be of help to them and to their child. Find out if the mental health care provider has worked with children the same age as your child. Some therapists work more with adolescents or preschoolers, for example, while others work with the whole age range. Ask about willingness to coordinate care with school psychologists, your pediatrician, protective services workers and others involved in the life of your child. While the content of therapy sessions is confidential, with your written permission the therapist can share information with other professionals. You should also find out how much of what is told to a therapist by your child the therapist will be willing to share with you. Some degree of confidentiality is crucial for your child to feel he or she can trust the therapist, and you should not expect full disclosure by the therapist of all that is said, especially when children are older. Therapists will generally reveal to parents issues of safety (danger to self and others) and must report to the child protective services any abuse of a child. Beyond that, each therapist likely has his or her own policies, and these should be clarified to make sure that they are comfortable to the parent and child. Many therapists ask the child at the end of an individual session, "Of what we talked about today, what would you like me to share with your parents and what would you like me to keep private?" Then they go with the child's preference unless it crosses the lines mentioned above. Younger children tend to say it is OK to tell their parents everything, while older children are more likely to want privacy on issues that they are not yet ready to have revealed. Confidentiality and respect for boundaries are especially important in the treatment of issues related to child sexual abuse because the offense involved the crossing of boundaries and violation of trust.

Christian families often wonder how important it is to seek out a therapist who is also a believer. For some problem areas—and child sexual abuse is one—where core issues of forgiveness, guilt, anger at God, self-worth and the like are at stake, a therapist who shares the belief system of the family seeking help is often preferable. A mature Christian therapist grounded in Scripture and experienced in walking out his or her faith can bring special comfort and wisdom to a family or child dealing with the aftermath of abuse. This comfort will transcend what psychotherapy alone can offer; it will blend the insights of clinical training with the truths of God's ways. The advantage of working with a fellow believer is found in a shared reference system and a common belief in the presence and action of God in the lives of the child and family. Even with a Christian therapist, however, it is necessary to be clear about your preference for praying together or not, referring to Scripture or not, contacting your minister or not. There are many different denominations and practices within the Christian world and room for a lot of misunderstanding even between well-meaning believers, so it is good to be explicit about what you want and expect. When the abuse has occurred in the context of Christian care (when the perpetrator is a youth or music minister, for instance), it may be best to de-emphasize the explicitly Christian aspects of treatment, as they may replicate aspects of the abuse.

When no Christian professional is available, it is often possible to find a good therapist willing to work within the framework of the client's faith, even if he or she is not a believer. God can work his healing grace through those who do not name his name. Some direction from the client about what is or is not acceptable may be needed if the therapist suggests techniques or perspectives with which the client is not comfortable, but this may happen even with a Christian provider. As with issues discussed above, there is no way to know without asking. All therapists at centers or practices with Christian names are not necessarily Christian, and many therapists at secular agencies or with practices that are not identified as Christian may be.

Whether to visit a male or female therapist is a matter of personal preference. Adolescent clients often find it easier to talk to someone of the same sex, although this is not a hard and fast rule. For some children, seeing a therapist who is the same sex as the perpetrator is very difficult; for others, it is a very healing experience. A good therapist will be sensitive to this issue and willing to discuss it openly and help a family evaluate whether or not it is an issue in their case. If the child states a preference as to male or female therapist, talk with the child to understand his or her reason. Then, if the choices in your area allow it, go with the child's preference.

Cost can also be a significant factor in choosing a therapist. As mentioned above, finding a therapist who is on your insurance company's list of approved therapists may make a difference in the out-of-pocket cost. Each family has to weigh for itself the relative importance of several factors—the cost of the therapist, his or her experience, and whether or not he or she is a Christian. Some insurance companies specifically ask providers if they provide Christian counseling and can give members a list of mental health providers who say that they provide this service. Community mental health clinics, child guidance centers and other not-for-profit agencies may also be available in your community to help at a reduced fee. Often these agencies offer experienced therapists who have made a professional career choice to make their services available to those who cannot afford to pay full fee. It may also be possible to see a student in training who has the benefit of the most recent theory and practice and the supervision of a licensed professional—sort of two for the price of one. If finding a Christian therapist is an important consideration for your family, do not overlook these agencies. If you call and ask, they will tell you if any of their staff provide this service—sometimes believers choose to work at such agencies to provide their services to those who cannot afford to pay private practice fees.

What Happens Once You Get There?
Suppose that you have selected a therapist and are coming in for a first visit. What can you expect to happen?

If you are seeking help for a child, clarify whether or not to bring the child with you on the first visit. Many child therapists prefer to meet only with the parents or adult guardians on the first visit to collect background information and do paperwork without the child being present. This allows the adults freedom to talk openly in a way that they may not feel comfortable doing in front of the child. The first experience the child has with the therapist can then be positive rather than a rehash of the concerns and problems that the family is having. An exception to this policy is often made with adolescents: if they are not present from the beginning, they may feel that the adults have ganged up on them and talked about them behind their backs.

The first visit is often a review of history, both the abuse incidents and other developmental and medical facts, and a general fact-finding session. The therapist is seeking to know the child's family and social situations. Parents or guardians can also take advantage of this first session to ask questions to get to know the therapist better. Some therapists draw a strict line between their private and professional lives and will not reveal any information about themselves, since the focus needs to be on the family with whom they are speaking and not on them. Others will give general information about themselves, such as whether they are married and whether they have children, to help families know that their experience is practical as well as theoretical. All information shared should be in the service of the child and his or her family, however. A therapy relationship loses its effectiveness if it becomes too chummy, so do not be offended by your counselor's keeping a professional distance. Do not be afraid to ask questions, but be aware that if you do not get answers to some of what you ask, the reason may be based on counseling theory rather than on the therapist's having something to hide.

A first visit with a child will often include a verbal interview and time for play. Depending on the age of the child and the approach taken by the therapist, more or less of the time spent with the child will be spent in play or verbal exchanges. By watching the child's play, paying attention to what happens and why, and making interventions in the medium of play selected by the child, the therapist may be able to gain insights into the child's perspective on the abuse experience and how the child is processing it. Some children will talk directly about what has happened to them, others only symbolically in play. Feel free to ask the therapist about his or her approach and reasons for taking that particular road with children.

Once therapy begins, the concerns that brought a child or adult into treatment will be discussed. Any of the issues considered at the opening of this chapter might be delved into in more detail. Roots in the past might be unearthed. Present ambivalence that leads to working in two directions at once and thus self-sabotaging might be explored. Irrational ideas that limit and defeat even a believer who knows the truth of Christ that is meant to set us free might be uncovered and corrected. While the direction taken will differ from therapist to therapist according to theoretical orientation and the differing needs of various clients, some similar themes will be explored. Guilt and blame can often cripple recovery, both for the child victim and for other family members. Forgiveness is often a key to emotional healing. Openness and secrecy are often issues that need to be addressed, as are trust and betrayal. All of these may need to be considered in relationship to the abuser, to the child, to family members and to God.

How Long Should Therapy Last?

Families often wonder how they will know when it is time to stop mental health treatment. This is usually clear to both the therapist and the person coming to treatment. The specific issue about which therapy was begun may be resolved. (Suzie no longer has nightmares, or her mother is not ashamed to go to PTA meetings anymore.) Other times enough insight has been obtained or enough techniques for handling a problem mastered that both the therapist and the client (or family, in the case of a child) think that it is time to stop and allow the client to try managing life without an external coach.

If both the client and the therapist feel that no further progress is being made and it is time to stop, then it is usually time to do so, often with the thought that treatment could be resumed at a later date if it seemed necessary. Treatment ordered by the court needs to continue until the terms of the court order are met.

When the therapist and the family are in agreement that it is time for treatment to wind down and stop, time must be given for careful appropriate termination. Many child sexual abuse survivors have already felt pain at the sudden loss of a person with whom they are emotionally as well as physically intimate—when the secret came out and the abuser disappeared from their lives. Care must be taken that the therapist not disappear in a similar sudden manner. The child must be helped to see why termination is necessary and why it is a good thing—a sign of growth and the ability to stand on one's own two feet—and not a punishment for doing something wrong or a loss of a support. This can take several sessions and is an important part of the therapy and healing for children.

Therapy can and does help many people—both children and adults—to deal with the aftermath of child sexual abuse. One of the most difficult issues for the Christian to deal with—one he or she may or may not feel comfortable discussing with a counselor—is the question about why God allows such suffering to occur. This and other theological considerations are the focus of the next chapter.

6

Why Does God
Let This Happen?

Theological Questions
Raised by Children & Families

"Marge?"

"What, Tom?"

"I've been thinking about what happened to Suzie. Why does God let kids get hurt like this?"

"I don't know, Tom. Maybe we did some things wrong, and it's some kind of punishment for us. I don't see how God could be punishing a five-year-old."

"I figured God just wasn't able to stop it—like he's not all-powerful after all. Or maybe he doesn't really care about us like the church always said he did."

"Whatever it is, I just know I don't trust God like I did. I wish I could, but I don't. Do you think he's mad at me for that?"

"Hope not, because I'd be in trouble too!"

Christians who learn that children they know and love have been sexually abused frequently ask questions like these. Ministers, counselors, Sunday school teachers, family members and others who are trusted and loved may be privileged to share their struggle as they seek answers that are true to their experience of God, their understanding of the faith, and the depth of the pain that they feel after seeing what has happened to the children. Many never ask the questions but lock them away inside where they fester and may end up destroying what was once a vibrant walk with God. Children have their own questions and difficulties reconciling their experience with what they have believed about God. Those who seek to be of help to abused children and their families in a Christian context need to be prepared to walk alongside their sisters and brothers in Christ as they seek answers. This chapter, after an initial discussion of the importance of these questions and how best to address them, will consider six of the most common questions in the light of biblical data and the psychological realities faced by those asking the questions.

Some people who are dealing with child sexual abuse seek to shut off the questions that arise about God and how the abuse has changed their relationship with him. They may believe that to question the workings of God demonstrates a lack of faith. Or their emotions seem so overwhelming that they wonder if even God can handle the way they feel. Some wistfully express admiration for people they have heard of who experienced great tragedy and never even once asked God why. Yet the biblical authors show us real people in Scripture who question, struggle and cry out to God. It is still true today that more healing is accomplished with honesty before God, and answers can be found for those who courageously ask the hard questions.

The cry "How long, O LORD, how long?" goes up from his people throughout the history of the Jewish people. Jonah questioned the destruction of a shade plant, and Job had his moment to address his concerns to God. God responded, though his answers were perhaps more challenging than comforting. Far from condemning the questions, God was willing and able to provide answers. The book of Psalms is full of the outpouring of emotions before God. (In fact, praying some of the psalms and personalizing their laments can be very healing for those dealing with child sexual abuse.) Jesus' followers were free with their questions and feelings—whether wondering why a man was born blind or expressing doubt about the resurrection. Again Jesus had mercy and answered the concerns. We as his people today need to learn from this example and feel free to ask why. We need to be honest with ourselves, with each other and with God.

A difficulty many have today—and perhaps the prevalence of therapy has inadvertently contributed to this problem—is the belief that the question is more important than the answer; the process is of greater value than the end result. Questions and process *are* important, and one of the ways we show respect to people as we seek to help them is to value both their questions and the quality of our interaction with them. But Christians must avoid the temptation to hang on to the question too long after an answer has been provided through Scripture and the counsel of others. An answer that is hard to accept may still be the right one, and, even in the midst of listening and caring, we must be careful as Christian helpers to be true to the biblical data and provide accurate answers as best as we can.

When people share their deep questions, we must be careful how we respond. People take a risk in exposing their doubts and fears at a time when they are already feeling vulnerable. We must be gentle with them. Applaud their ability to face difficult questions. Ask what answers they have already considered and rejected, and why. Gauge their willingness to enter into dialogue. Better to simply lend a listening ear and leave a door open for future conversations rather than come on too strong with a response—even a biblically correct one—and lose the opportunity to continue ministry and be a part of God's healing in that person's life.

Having looked at some cautions and considerations regarding how to handle the questions when they arise, let us now turn to the tough questions that often come up for those dealing with child sexual abuse in a Christian context.

Question 1: Why Does God Let These Things Happen?

The "why?" question is as current as today's headlines and as old as people's relationship with God. As we seek to help those who struggle with real tragedy in life—including but not limited to child sexual abuse—we must approach the question with humility and the realization that the answer is not fully knowable this side of eternity. "My thoughts are not your thoughts, neither are your ways my ways," says God in Isaiah 55:8. Yet we do have some clues to what may be going on in the words of Scripture that we can offer to those struggling with this issue.

We know, for instance, that God desires good for his people. "I know the plans I have for you . . . plans for your welfare and not for harm," declares God (Jer 29:11 NRSV). While these words were spoken for a particular people at a particular point in salvation history, many have found comfort in the suggestion that God is not the author of their destruction or harm. Yet even for many who accept that God desires our good, the question must be asked why he allows evil to befall his people and especially innocents such as children who have been sexually abused.

This question seeks to plumb the motives of God, but the answer is not found there. Rather we must seek to know the person of God and what he desires for the people he has created. An understanding of who he is changes the question and allows us to move forward in considering the original issue. God has always allowed sin, yet Scripture clearly teaches that he hates evil. So what might he value so much that he would allow sin to occur and damage innocent people? He desires that people should love him with all their heart, all their mind and all their strength, and love their neighbors as themselves. He tells Israel that he does not desire burnt sacrifices but rather the offering of a contrite heart and humble spirit, and he requires his people "to act justly and to love mercy and to walk humbly with [their] God" (Mic 6:8). In these passages and elsewhere the consistent challenge of Scripture is to choose to walk after God's ways and not to follow the deceitfulness of our own hearts. God does not allow evil per se; he allows humans the choice of evil or good. Many, unfortunately, choose evil. And the evil that they choose has consequences for others—in the case of child sexual abuse, children and their families. The question is not, then, why God allows evil, but why people choose not to seek after God and his ways and instead follow their own desires—even when doing so wounds others, often those whom they love most deeply—and what is to be done about the sorry state of humanity.

Paul summarizes this dilemma by personalizing it in Romans 7:19-25: "What I do is not the good I want to do; no, the evil I do not want to do— this I keep on doing. . . . Who will rescue me from this body of death? Thanks be to God—through Jesus Christ." Child sexual abuse and the other horrors that plague us in the world are specific instances of sin. And God allows them as the down side of the choice that he desires all to make to turn toward him. Those who do not turn toward God seldom stay neutral and often turn away. And in the turning away they hurt others. Much pain and suffering flow out of not seeking his ways as he would desire. God hates sin more than we do, and the damaging of his children holds a special place of infamy for him; yet he must allow it or the call to holiness would not be a real choice.

The underlying questions for many whom I have seen are "Does God care?" and "If God cares, why doesn't he make it better?" The answers are "Of course" and "He is." There is his promise that "in all things God works for the good of those who love him, who have been called according to his purpose" (Rom 8:28). This promise can bring comfort to those suffering emotional pain and spiritual anguish due to child sexual abuse. Often the how and why are not readily visible in the midst of the difficulties of coping with child sexual abuse. But that is where faith comes in. We do not pretend that there is no pain or no evil deed has been done, but we hold on to the conviction that good will come out of it at some point down the road. And we keep walking forward, secure in the fact that God is walking the road with us and he knows the end right from the beginning (Is 46:10).

The end that he knows is laid out in the book of Revelation. Christians are headed for the new Jerusalem, where "there will be no more death or mourning or crying or pain" (Rev 21:4). While care must be taken not to offer only the solace of peace after death, those offering Christian counsel can put the pain of the present in the context of eternity and remind those who are suffering that this life is, after all, only transitory, and the eternal rewards will far outweigh any current suffering. We are being shaped for all eternity by what we experience in this lifetime. While this does not explain why God allows suffering to happen, it does point out that he uses it to perfect us for this life and the next. When evil does occur—and it will, as the result of bad choices made by women and men—God will find ways to use it for good.

Question 2: Is God Punishing the Child or the Adults?

Many families ask themselves what they (or the child victim) might have done to bring the tragedy of abuse down upon them. If there is an area of current or past sin in their lives, they may conclude that God has used the abuse as a means of judgment and punishment. If there is no apparent reason for punishment, many people wrongly conclude that there must be some unknown reason why they deserved to have this happen. They keep looking for that reason by going over the issue again and again. These patterns of thought are destructive and hinder healing. They can and should be challenged.

If the family with whom you are working looks to the Bible as a teaching authority, then you can turn with them to John 9, where Jesus and the disciples discuss an issue of who is to blame for a tragedy affecting a seemingly innocent victim. There was a man who was born blind, and the disciples wanted to know who was responsible. "Who has sinned, the man or his parents, that he was born blind?" they ask Jesus. Jesus does not affix blame. Instead, he changes the focus of the discussion. "Neither, it is so that the glory of God may be revealed," he tells his disciples. He points to the heart of the matter. Given that the man is now blind, speculation as to the possible sinful behavior that may have led to it is fruitless. The disciples instead need to be on the lookout for how the glory of God will be revealed.

In this case Jesus reaches out his hand and heals the person immediately. This may happen to a child who has been abused as well. Or God may use another route to healing that involves counseling, prayer, emotional support and the passage of time. However he heals, speculation as to the sin of the victim or family members will not lead to a quicker or longer-lasting cure.

There may be times when the victim or family needs to look at what they may have done to contribute the abuse. This is not to say that they are responsible—the perpetrator must bear the weight of responsibility for the choices made and actions taken against a child. Nor is it to say that they were somehow spiritually deficient, and so God allowed a child to be abused as a wake-up call. Parents and family members (and to some degree the child) need to ask, however, what went wrong and what could be done differently in the future so that the likelihood of abuse is lowered. This process can be very empowering both for the victim and his or her family. A counselor can help a family understand that the abuse was not set up by God to punish for past sins; that does not release them from the need to examine their actions that may have contributed to the abuse. But that comes later. The false idea of God as a vengeful deity who was just waiting for the chance to hit them with abuse needs to be dispelled so that they can turn to him for support as they walk through this difficult time.

Question 3: How Come I Can't Trust God Anymore?

Many people who have had a child abused—a son or daughter or another child for whom they care—experience a loss of trust in God. Most will have been praying for the protection of the child who was abused, and they may wonder what good their prayers did since God allowed the abuse. Those to whom this sort of tragedy is new are likely to have their faith stretched and maybe even broken by dealing with the reality that God could allow such abuse to occur to a child. If they have always looked to him for protection and never before been disappointed by him, then this event may crush their trust in God. Those who are new to the faith or whose Christian life has never had many bumps are especially vulnerable.

When counseling with people who have lost trust in God, a first step is to listen while they talk about how they lost it. Most will recite a story of trusting and then being disappointed as God seemingly failed to take their needs seriously or ignored their prayers. This loss of trust can be profound for some who feel as if the ground has disappeared beneath their feet. Don't rush in too quickly with biblical platitudes, or you run the risk of their feeling that you have not taken their despair seriously. However, you need not leave them in the midst of their darkness without offering some hope. After listening, remind them of truths about God's faithfulness that they already know but are not currently feeling. Point out that long-lasting trust in God is based on what we know, not only on what we feel. Encourage them to go along for the ride with their feelings, to recognize and acknowledge them, but not always to believe them as a source of accurate information. Reassure them that it is normal to go through a period of distrust after such a trial and that this all-too-human reaction does not disqualify them from all that God has for them.

Trust can grow again as a family remembers how God has been faithful in the past and sees again in the present how he is currently faithful. We may never know why God has allowed certain dreadful events to happen, but we can know with certainty that he will continue to work out his good purpose for all of his children. As families see that truth played out in their lives, they will begin to trust again.

A special case of this problem may occur when a child has been abused by his or her father and has great difficulty with the concept of a heavenly Father, since that word implies broken promises, pain and betrayal. Others who do not have these sinister associations to the word may seek to bring comfort by talking about God as a loving father. This will do more harm than good. For some, it may be useful to point out that God can be the sort of father that their human father failed to be. An adolescent may be able to understand that his or her human father was supposed to represent the love of God and that, though the human father failed, the adolescent can approach God directly and receive God's love despite the inadequate model that he or she experienced. People in this situation will need time, prayer and the opportunity to talk about their conflicts between who they know God to be and how they feel about God.

Question 4: Has God Abandoned Me?

Along with a lack of trust, many people who go through the theological aftermath of child sexual abuse feel abandoned by God. Some reason that God is punishing them, others that God is not able to protect the innocent children, so what hope do they have as sinners? Others feel so dirty or unworthy because of having been molested that they are sure that God could not tolerate being with them any longer. Some question the whole Christian faith, so shaken are they by the trauma of what they have experienced.

The Bible is clear that God in no way abandons his people. He is "an ever-present help in trouble," we are told in Psalm 46:1. Nothing can separate us from God's love, Paul remind us in Romans 8. These facts are realities even when they do not *feel* true. The problem is not then so much that God has abandoned his people in their distress but that his people may feel abandoned. This problem may be approached in three ways:

Help people understand biblically that they are not alone. Sometimes that knowledge will in and of itself give the support needed to keep going on. The biblical teaching that God never abandons his people has been hinted at already. God is a God of covenant. First the Jewish people and now Christians through the death of Jesus on the cross have a covenant with God that he will be our God and we will be his people. This covenant is based on God's initiative, begun by his call and maintained by his love. He must remain true to himself, and part of that is to remain true to commitment to his people.

Challenge a reliance upon feelings. While people may feel they are alone, that does not make it so, and feeling alone does not change the requirements of the Christian life or the fact that God provides what we need to move in obedience. Sometimes people respond well to a reframing of tragedy as a challenge or opportunity to rise to more than they thought they could. Feeling abandoned by God is a natural reaction to awful circumstances, but it need not make a Christian response to those circumstances impossible. Feelings can be influenced by fatigue, ongoing stress, clinical depression or anxiety in response to the trauma of child sexual abuse. Realizing that fact may set people free to live beyond their feelings and to watch and pray while their feelings catch up with their obedience to God. This is not a call to a denial of feelings but rather a reminder that while feelings may shape our perception of our reality, they are not the reality itself. Our culture has distorted this truth, leading too many to believe that their feelings are reality instead of just a response to what is real. Seeing this difference can have a profound impact on the believer who *feels* abandoned by God and therefore believes that he or she *is* abandoned. When believers realize that their feelings can mislead them, they are set free to look at the roots of their feelings and what it is in their lives that maintains their false beliefs about themselves and God. This can lead to change that will help to restore communion with God.

Provide the living presence of Jesus in his body, the church, to assure people that they are not alone. God loves and provides for people and meets real needs in the present moment in his name. Sometimes people feel abandoned by God because God's people have neglected them. We are his hands and feet on earth now. If we meet them and care for them in Jesus' name, they are more likely to know that he is with them too. People can and should turn back to their church communities for support at a time of difficulty in their lives, even if they have walked away previously. Some congregations are better than others in giving compassionate care in Jesus' name. But each of us, as we seek to be of help to a child or family member dealing with child sexual abuse, must remember that we are an ambassador of God in that specific place at that specific time.

Question 5: Is God Angry at Me or Can He Forgive Me for Feeling This Way?

When people feel abandoned by God, disappointed in how he has behaved in allowing evil acts to be done or even angry at him, they often feel that they need to hide these feelings from him. This may be because God's people have done a poor job in helping others to work through these feelings. All too often believers are told "Don't say such a thing about God!" as if it would come as a surprise to God to find out that someone has such feelings. Or it may have to do with the projection of human rules of relationship (especially from the families people grew up in) onto the relationship with God. Rather than seeing God as the author of all creation and knowing how to relate to him as he desires, people often see God as a reflection of their own imperfect mothers and fathers. If they came from a family where anger could not be expressed, disappointment could not be voiced and became the norm, or abandonment was felt and never discussed, they will believe that the same rules apply with God. Opening their minds and hearts to the reality that God is big enough to handle their feelings (in fact, may be the only one big enough to fully handle their feelings) can be the beginning of healing.

Biblical authors knew this truth, often lost to contemporary believers. People overwhelmed by their feelings about God and his people but unsure that they are allowed to express them should be encouraged to read the book of Psalms. The author pours out every human feeling. Sometimes the psalm itself documents how telling God can change the feeling. We have this record to encourage us to do the same.

So, far from being angry, God desires that you to tell him how you feel. For he knows that in the telling you are opening up yourself to his love and the presence of his Spirit that can bring about healing and change. God is not mad for how you feel. And he will forgive the feelings to whatever degree they need to be forgiven, if you ask him to do so. They may not need forgiving. Honest emotions based on what we know at the time seldom do. But they may need transformation. Our judgments of God are based only on our imperfect human knowledge, and the feelings that flow from them are similarly limited. As we understand better, feelings can change. People may move from anger to sorrow that they misjudged God. If so, he will forgive that. Or they may stay at anger or disappointment for a long time. Then God responds as did Jesus on the cross, with forgiveness that we act out of ignorance. Sin angers God, as does disobedience. But feelings do not, and forgiveness is freely given.

Question 6: Will It Ever Get Any Better?

Some people move through the theological questions considered in this chapter quickly. They may be able to stand so firmly on the rock of their faith that they never slip off into the quagmire of doubt, pain and confusion that so many, both children and adults, fall into when faced with the life-changing fact of child sexual abuse. This need not be a reflection of their goodness, knowledge or superior grasp of theology, though those who do fall into the quagmire often feel inferior in each of these areas. As they deal with the questions they have or with reactions that seem ungodly and unexpected, they are also dealing with shameful feelings that they are bad or wrong for even being in this place. These are the people who see no way out, who feel worse than they ever thought a Christian could for longer than they ever thought they could endure. Some cannot stand it and have a psychiatric breakdown; others leave their faith behind. Those who keep enduring ask if it is ever going to get any better. The answer is two-fold—in the short term, probably, with work; in the long term, definitely, by God's grace.

In this world we are not promised happiness. There is no absolute guarantee that it will get better. Time tends to heal. Other activities crowd out pain. The black fog lifts, and the sun shines again. Yet Jesus reminded the disciples that "in the world you will have trouble." When people despair at feeling separated from God, in the midst of a psychological depression and a spiritual desert, we can point them toward practices and principles that will help them out of the valley (and the next chapter considers how to do exactly that), but we must not promise a quick fix or devalue them by discounting the depth of their pain. They may feel doubly bad that they are not even able to heal correctly, or perhaps, feeling misunderstood, they may dismiss the person who seeks to help as shallow and uncaring. The road that leads out of the depths of despair can be long and dark, and we must support those who walk it even as we continue to encourage them that there is light at the end of the road and fellowship with God and his people even while they walk in darkness.

The long-term outlook—viewed from the longest perspective possible, eternity—is a good one. The picture of the New Jerusalem in the book of Revelation, the ultimate destination for all believers, is of a land where there is no more sorrow or grief, no more tears or crying as described in Revelation 21. While some may dismiss promises of reward after death, many who find life's circumstances unbearable receive tremendous comfort from the fact that this life is only temporary. Compared with eternity, the pain we bear now is short-lived. Even if a parent or abuse victim never overcomes the tremendous wounding he or she experiences in this lifetime, there is the promise of "a new heaven, a new earth," where justice prevails and pain ceases. There Jesus, who has overcome even the final enemy, death, will bring in the fullness of his kingdom, and all those who suffer will be restored.

7

How Does God Bring Healing?

Methods & Manners of Healing for Child Sexual Abuse

"I know that we should be open-minded to whatever would help Bobby heal, but I wonder what's really the right course for us now."

"It's so hard to know. His youth minister is recommending prayer and sticking around Christian kids who are a good influence, but his counselor seems to think that the group for boys who have been abused would help him. I can't get over worrying that hearing their stories—maybe worse things than he went through himself—will only make it harder."

"But he says he never feels 'normal' around 'regular' kids. Maybe it would help him to see that other kids who have been through the same thing look and act normal—at least that's what Dr. Kyle says."

"Dr. Kyle has done a good job with Bobby, but he's not a believer—I don't

think so anyway—and I don't know where he stands with the spiritual side of things. Do you think it's out of line to ask? I mean, just what would they talk about in the group and what kind of advice would they give? Do we want Bobby exposed to that?"

 "Let's pray about it, them maybe talk to Bart and Suzie. I know that their daughter Amy was in counseling for a while, and maybe they have worked through some of these questions."

The parents portrayed in this vignette are asking good questions about how to steer a course that will help their son Bobby recover from his abusive experiences. Seeking to use resources of their Christian community and the best that modern science has to offer may leave a family putting together their own unique, hybrid program of counseling, prayer, Bible study, medication and more. This chapter looks at some components that God might use to bring about restoration and healing, and it considers guidelines on how to put together a specific program at a specific time for the needs of a specific child.

Healing—from brokenness, disease and sin—and the movement toward wholeness are themes throughout all of Scripture. In the Old Testament record of the dealings of *Jehovah Rapha,* "the God who heals," with his people, we find stories of prophets who proclaim God's intentions to bring redress for societal sin and personal deliverance from the results of individual brokenness and separation from God. At times individuals are prayed for and healed as well. These stories have metaphorical meaning as types of God's redemptive workings in Israel, but they also illustrate the heart of God—to be at work bringing about healing and restoration. Jesus' earthly ministry is full of examples of healing, such as the blind man at the pool of Bethsaida, Jairus's daughter, the woman with the issue of blood and the paralytic lowered through the roof by his friends. Some of these provided teaching opportunities for Jesus or illustrate aspects of God's love in symbolic form to the church today. Additionally they reveal the healing heart of God. Scripture notes repeatedly that Jesus was "moved with compassion" at the sight of those needing healing. When he commissioned his disciples to go forth in his name, healing the sick was one of the charges given to them. If Hebrews 13:8 is to be believed, then Jesus is the same yesterday, today and forever, and it remains his intention to bring healing to the world today.

If God desires to reach out and heal the wounded and broken—those in physical, mental and spiritual pain—how does he do so now when Jesus is no longer walking the earth in a human body to reach out and touch with his own hands? The book of Acts and the Epistles illustrate that the theology and practice of the early church continued to stress the dual themes of prayer and dependence upon God to move by the power of his Spirit in Jesus' name to accomplish miracles and healing. And the early church emphasized the need for Jesus' followers to speak the words of life, touch in prayer the wounded, and in concrete ways meet the needs of those who are broken in body, mind and spirit. The care of the widows needed to be taken seriously in Acts 6, but the disciples needed to attend to preaching the word, so deacons were appointed to meet the daily physical needs of the widows. As Paul outlines the functioning of the church as parallel to the functioning of a physical body, a picture emerges of how the body of Christ can and should operate: all members use their gifts to meet the specific needs they are gifted to address, without argument over which function is superior or inferior, as in 1 Corinthians 12. We need to value the gifting of each believer and seek to understand how it can be applied to bring about God's best for individuals in need of healing.

Many contemporary churches are out of balance in this matter—elevating only preaching or healing or counseling, forgetting that a healthy body serves many functions. This unbalance, which is so easy to fall into, can be confusing to families seeking healing for their children or themselves in the aftermath of child sexual abuse, for they may believe that they need only to hear the word preached and be saved, or only to be prayed for regularly with the laying on of hands, or only to be delivered from demonic spirits. God has never worked his healing in this one-dimensional way. The biblical data shows that Jesus himself used different means in different situations to bring about wholeness, and we should expect the church today to consider all the means available for healing. This requires wisdom and discernment. Not all of the interventions available are best for any one person, and some may not be wise for Christians at all. Valuable counsel can be obtained from ministers, elders, and wise men and women of God who have thought about these issues and dealt with similar problems before.

Some people get caught up in a dichotomy between Christian and non-Christian methodologies that can be distracting and counterproductive. God can and does use all sorts of interventions to bring healing. While it is true that some interventions that may not be specifically Christian need to be augmented with solid biblical teaching, it can also be true that Christian programming that hits the mark with most people misses when it come to the special needs of sexually abused children. All approaches need to be carefully considered and monitored to make sure that they are bringing about healing and not deepening the problems already caused by the abuse. Among the many possible avenues of healing, seven are listed below with comments on how each can help and hurt in the case of child sexual abuse:

Sunday school/youth groups have the advantage of being the "natural setting" for children to learn about God, the Christian life, sin and forgiveness, and other basics of the Christian faith. Standard Sunday school curricula may not touch directly on topics related to sexual abuse, but many of the conditions discussed in earlier chapters will emerge in a group of children and could be recognized and addressed by an abuse-aware teacher or minister. (Some details of how to help a church become more abuse-proactive will be discussed in chapter nine.) Issues such as forgiveness when someone has done something wrong to you, feeling dirty and separated from God (and the solution offered by confession and absolution), knowing your worth in Christ, and the fallacy of hopelessness for the Christian can all be addressed without mentioning child sexual abuse. And in addressing these common abuse-related issues, teachers will find that they are also answering questions others have. Sexually abused children sometimes withdraw from social settings out of fear of being found out or because of their own feelings of being different. Participating in a Sunday school class or youth group where they are accepted and feel "part of the gang" can be very healing.

Difficulties with pursuing healing in natural settings such as Sunday school classes or youth groups may include the fact that many children who have been sexually abused feel different than their peers and will not mix well with others. (Or if they do, they may reject the potentially healing messages offered by saying to themselves, *This is true for everyone else except me.*) Others may begin to talk about their abusive experience, which may be hard for the group to handle. A wise teacher or youth leader will intervene with caution here in a way that supports the youth or child revealing the information and yet protects the others from having to bear more than children can be expected to carry. Those children who are reacting to abuse by acting out sexually do not belong in a setting where their presence may put other children at risk and should not be included in these church activities without careful planning and supervision by the adults in charge.

Worship services/sacraments/prayer can be very moving and life-changing for child sexual abuse survivors and their families. Those feeling angry and alienated from God may find themselves drawn back into fellowship with him in the familiar setting of the worship service. The Holy Spirit may directly touch the hearts of wounded, frightened or angry people in worship in ways that the words or actions of other people could never accomplish. The sacraments may bring an awareness of the reality of God that transcends words, thoughts or feelings. Prayers can effectively channel the power of God and bring further healing in body, mind and spirit.

Difficulties with this format occur also. Some may never make it into a church for a worship service. Those who are angry at God or his people may stay far away from the place that they see as the home of hypocrisy or a gathering-place for those who have damaged them. Even in carefully crafted liturgies designed to bring those participating closer to God, words may be used or songs sung that cause further hurt for a child or family still recovering from child sexual abuse. A prayer for protection may remind of times when protection was lacking. A song about "the joy we have in Jesus" or some other seemingly innocuous topic may bring condemnation to someone feeling depressed and blaming themselves for not being able to know the presence of God as they once did. A careless word or deed perceived as judgmental by someone overly sensitive to rejection or judgment due to child sexual abuse may drive that person away from the church and the healing it could offer. Prayers that appear not to be answered may confirm an abuse survivor's feeling of being unloved even by God. There are times when attending the worship service or seeking prayer may be the last thing a person ought to do. The body of believers may continue to pray for those who are not present with great impact (even without naming names), and that may be the best way to move forward at times.

Bible study, both individual and corporate, can be an important source of healing. Knowledge of the Word of God, and through it of the way of God with people, can serve as an important corrective to the kind of false and unhealthy thinking that is often part of the aftermath of child sexual abuse. Some of these corrective ideas from Scripture have been discussed in an earlier chapter. Recognizing, for example, that God does not inflict such tragedy as punishment for sin, or that no sin, however vile, can separate us from the love of God, can help combat common erroneous ideas. The strength to persevere can also be found in reading 1 Peter on the importance of holding on to the faith or in Paul's call to fight the good fight (1 Tim 6:12) and see the race through to the end. The author of Hebrews encourages us to persevere (Heb 12:1). As 2 Timothy 3:16 notes, the Scriptures play a very important role in the life of the believer, and this can be especially true when people turn to them for solace and instruction in the wake of abuse.

The drawbacks can also be important to consider. If people are likely to place themselves under condemnation, Bible study is an activity that is all too open to being used this way. Even long-term Christians with no specific trauma history can fall under the spell of believing that however much they read, it is not enough, or however well they understand the text, it is never truly accurate. There is a danger too that someone depressed or feeling alienated may misapply passages of Scripture to bolster this viewpoint and end up further from God after seeking to know him better through Scripture reading. The mental state and disposition of a person need to be assessed before suggesting that Scripture reading will be a healing intervention. Offering to meet with an individual for Bible study or checking in with a person after a group teaching to see what he or she is taking home from it may be one way to correct this tendency.

Mentoring/Big Brother-Big Sister programs can provide relationships and bonding that have been lost. Child sexual abuse can damage so much for children. Social relationships, self-image, understanding of God and more can be impacted by the immoral exploitation that they have suffered. It is hard to fathom the damage that can be done by one emotionally intimate relationship gone wrong. At times a carefully constructed corrective relationship can help to reestablish trust in others and deal with the damage done. It gives the child another person who will care for him or her—this time without hurting the child physically or emotionally. Being able to go camping again without fear that a man you feel close to will try to climb into your sleeping bag helps a child to understand that the problem was not within *him or her* but rather is in the abuser. Doing the same activities with another person who does not cross over the lines of appropriate behavior underlines for a child the truth that most people are not abusive and will not take advantage of emotionally intimate times by seeking to sexualize them. Living the experience will teach this more effectively than hearing it from others. A mentoring relationship can also be a place where fears and worries are addressed in naturally occurring friendships (as opposed to only with a professional therapist). Mentors can be specially selected and trained by pastoral staff to know how to provide a safe place and how to react when the sexualized issues emerge. At times the pastors themselves are able to be the mentors. Their involvement may be of special help to the child with nagging theological questions secondary to the abusive experience.

For some children, while the idea seems good in theory, the reality of forming another relationship that may mirror the abusive relationship and could become abusive itself is too difficult to undertake. They should not be forced or pressured into doing so, since such coercion mimics the dynamics of the abuse itself. Even with the best screening and training, there is a possibility that the mentoring relationship could become abusive, and this must be monitored closely. Sometimes group activities with a trusted Sunday school teacher or youth leader can have the same healing impact without exposing the child to the dangers (real or imaginary) of one-on-one contact.

The corporate life of the church—simply being a part of the family of God—can be very healing to someone who has felt damaged by abuse and unqualified for friendship and acceptance. Not only worship services and Bible studies but all aspects of the life of the body can be healing for someone who feared that he or she would never again fit in anywhere. Being asked to help out with chores or other tasks that need doing can boost an abuse survivor's self-image. Being joked with and treated like one of the crowd can erase the tapes that keep playing in a survivor's head if the abuser said that he or she was different or "a loser." Having responsibilities can overcome a sense of incompetence or a feeling that *No one will ever be able to trust me again after what happened.*

The dangers inherent in an abuse survivor's joining in fully with the life of a body of believers are the same as the source of the potential benefits—he or she is likely to be treated the same as everyone else. If there are lingering sensitivities due to the abuse, the occasionally thoughtless behavior of brothers and sisters in Christ might be personalized or seen as more meaningful than it is. This need not be a problem if the person is able to talk about it and clarify the issue. In fact, it could be a plus, but the awareness of the potential conflict should be there for those choosing to make this a part of a healing plan. Emotional processing or social skills that were compromised as a result of the abuse may not yet be fully healed. An abuse survivor might expect special treatment due to what he or she has been through. The person may even already be receiving special consideration from family and close friends and may be surprised when the body of believers treats him or her with the same expectations and requirements that they have for everyone else. Again, this could be a plus if handled correctly—but the individual entering into the community needs to think through how much he or she wishes to share about what has happened and the pros and cons of doing so. Generally, it will be best to keep quiet and cope with the help of family and a few close friends who know the history. If the past abuse is widely known, the person may find himself or herself labeled and ostracized in ways that are more reflective of the community's prejudices than of his or her own special needs.

Individual therapy can seem like a leap for many believers, for unless the therapist is also a Christian, taking this healing course may mean working with someone outside of the community of the faith. Even with a Christian therapist there may be concerns about the nature of psychology or the interventions suggested. For the purposes of this discussion it should be noted that God can use therapy to completely turn a child's life around in the space of six to twelve months. (On a personal note, I feel that the opportunity to participate in this process as God's agent for change is one of the most moving and thrilling therapy situations I have had the privilege of being in with a family.) Because of specialized training in the dynamics and aftermath of abuse, a qualified therapist can help a child and family through the predictable and painful healing steps needed for recovery from child sexual abuse. A therapist familiar with the research literature knows what has been shown to work and can save a family many trips down blind alleys. The therapist can also be an encouragement in the darker moments, especially if by virtue of his or her experience in helping many families the therapist can reassure them that things will get better and help them know what to do to make it so.

Dangers can involve trust, competency and potential conflicts with a family's religious values. Parents may have a difficult time trusting another adult to be alone with their child after the child has been abused—especially since the therapist is likely to be relatively unknown to the family (and they may have already been betrayed by someone they knew and trusted). A child may be frightened of the therapist or of the therapy process. When you look at it from the child's point of view, many aspects of therapy replicate the abusive environment—the child is alone, one on one with an adult behind closed doors, talking about sexualized things and with the explicit expectation that what happens in the room is "private and confidential." An experienced therapist will address these issues head on: invite the parents to stay in the room until the child and parents are both comfortable with a separation (except as discussed in chapter three, in the case of an evaluation where special legal concerns make this impossible); tell a child that he or she is free to talk to anyone the child would like to about what is said and done in the therapy session (thus explicitly differentiating it from the abusive episodes). Until a child and family feel comfortable with a therapist, they should not be rushed into trying to talk about issues they are not ready to discuss.

A well-meaning but inexperienced or untrained child therapist seeking to help a child and family deal with the trauma of sexual abuse and its aftermath can do tremendous damage. Even a Christian who bathes his or her work with prayer and seeks to counsel out of a compassionate heart can do damage. Parents should be certain that a potential counselor is, in fact, equipped for the job before starting treatment. It is always appropriate to ask about education and training, to inquire about licensing and to find out about how many families in similar situations a counselor has worked with prior to your own.

Threats to a family's beliefs are rare. A well-trained and sensitive therapist will seek to work within a family's religious system, even when it is not the same as his or her own. Misunderstandings and hurt feelings may occur, however, and the therapist and family should be prepared to talk them through as they happen. Even when the therapist is a fellow believer, there are many branches within the church, and one who is familiar with the ins and outs of the theology and practice of his or her own denomination may unknowingly step on the toes of another from a different tradition. Families should talk about the place of prayer in counseling, the use of Scripture and other issues so that they can be prepared to ask the counselor for what they want. They might also want to talk about their moral practices and how these might impact treatment—for instance, a family may prefer that common adult terms or technical names be used for genitalia should the abusive experiences be discussed in detail with a child, and they may prefer to avoid slang terms. Conversely, others may want to use only "family names" for genitalia and bodily processes and avoid the common adult terms or technical names.

Group therapy is a treatment that many parents—and many children as well—are uncomfortable with. Parents often worry that the other children in the group may have been more seriously abused than their own children and will talk about or do something that will further traumatize their child. Children worry about talking about their abusive experiences in front of others, feeling that the other group members will not like them because they have been abused. It can be difficult for children to fathom the fact that abuse has occurred with other children as well as themselves. When they grasp it, that fact alone can be a very healing event—they no longer see themselves as uniquely bad and unworthy. This is a primary motivation behind group therapy for child sexual abuse—helping children to see that they are not alone. Children also find that they can learn from the coping strategies of peers and may even be able to help a peer out with something that they have already learned for themselves. This boosts self-esteem. It is also effective as a therapy tool—children are more able to learn from each other than from adults, who are removed from them by age and experience. On the purely pragmatic front, groups can also be much more cost-effective, since a service provider can cover the same issues with a group of children in less time than it would take to see each of them individually.

Some children are, in fact, so overwhelmed by the details of the abuse that others have suffered that group therapy is not good for them. Others are abuse-reactive in their behavior or in some other way behaviorally unsuited for groups and should not be included in this approach. If the family is very leery of groups and too uncomfortable to feel they can support the child as he or she enters into the group experience, individual therapy may be indicated before, or instead of, group treatment.

Medication is indicated when there is an underlying physiological problem. This problem may predate the child sexual abuse (and possibly have been exacerbated by it) or may have developed following the abuse. Depression, anxiety, obsessive-compulsive behaviors, psychotic thought disturbances and bipolar disorders all respond well to medication. Without medication, the chances of major lasting improvement for people with these conditions are slim. Many of the same people who would take insulin without question to manage diabetes have difficulty with the notion of a psychotropic medication for psychiatric disturbance, feeling somehow that God would not approve of this intervention. There are no biblical grounds for this fear. There are drawbacks to all of the psychotropic medications;

these can and should be discussed with the psychiatric or prescribing physician prior to starting the treatment. Some of the side effects are temporary or minor; others are more serious and may last as long as the drugs are in use. Each individual must decide whether the side effects are worth it and are less debilitating to endure than the condition for which the medication is prescribed—or whether he or she would prefer to manage the disease without the medication because the cure seems worse than the original problem.

Self-help books (bibliotherapy) like this one and others addressing the issues of child sexual abuse and its aftermath can be of tremendous help to children and families struggling with the issues raised by this traumatic life event. Solid information about the issues to be dealt with and suggestions for how to do so can be found in good reading material. Many people who would be unwilling to go and talk to someone about their problems or the issues that their family faces, or who are not sure how to help a friend but want to learn how without having to discuss topics that they may find embarrassing, will find a part of the help that they need in self-help books.

The problem is that only a part of what is needed is found in such books. To the degree that they help a person turn to God or to others for help in sorting through issues and moving beyond where they are stuck in their own processing of issues, the books are helpful. To the degree that they may serve to further isolate an already isolated population and thus cause more alienation and vulnerability, they are not helpful.

Putting Together a Program That Works

Each family is left with the question: How is God seeking to heal my child and me at this point in time? Today's answer may not be tomorrow's answer as growth and healing accomplished today clear the road for a new intervention or growth point tomorrow. It is important to get a sense of priorities and think about what to tackle when. Life-threatening or dangerous issues come first; issues that put others at risk or expose the person to harm come next; school problems, social problems and self-image issues that will cause additional difficulties if not dealt with immediately should be handled next; concerns that have to do primarily with comfort or abstract questions can typically wait. Legally mandated treatment must be sought out immediately.

In addition to approaching healing by seeking to identify priorities and deal with first things first, families need to consider what is available in their communities and deal with those issues for which God has provided resources. If no group treatment for child sexual abuse is available, then the child with the issues typically targeted by a group will need to look at them individually, perhaps in conjunction with other affirming experiences with age mates, a mentoring program with caring and appropriate adults, and directed readings or other activities to provide the new ways of looking at thoughts and feelings that group exercises might otherwise accomplish.

The individual proclivities of a child need to be considered. (An outgoing child, for instance, might find a group easier than an introvert, who may need three months of individual treatment with one of the group therapists first before he or she feels comfortable enough to enter the group.) The family's comfort level with discussing abuse-related issues or dealing with non-Christian providers of service, as well as other issues, will also influence their choices as they develop a plan of action that will lead to healing.

All the choices made in developing such a plan should be made in prayer and with input from those who know the child and other adults in the family system. Those seeking healing for their children and themselves should not forget Proverbs 11:14, which reminds us of the value of many counselors.

Two brief vignettes show how the healing plans developed by the families of children who experienced similar abusive acts can be very different to address differing situations.

Lucy is a seven-year-old girl who has been sexually abused by her uncle for the past four years. The abuse started with showering together and led to both anal and vaginal digital (finger or object) and penile penetration. Lucy's uncle would insist that they pray together before and after the abusive episodes, and he said God wanted him to teach her about a special way of being close to a man because he loved her so much. Her parents first noticed that something was wrong when Lucy refused to pray with them anymore before bed and told them that God really didn't take care of children because when you prayed, bad things happened. Lucy is withdrawn, her appetite has dwindled, and she is losing weight. She is not sleeping well, has lost interest in her scout troop and is no longer willing to attend the dance lessons she used to love.

Many important issues jump out of Lucy's story and illustrate the need to proceed on several levels at once. She is clearly depressed—appetite disturbance, weight loss, lack of interest in previously enjoyed activities, and sleep disturbance are red flags. She needs a good medical evaluation and possibly antidepressant medications. Her misconceptions about God and prayer need to be addressed in a sensitive way that shows understanding for how her uncle misused the trust that she had in him and distorted her understanding of prayer and of God himself. Looking at God's Word with a trusted adult (in an age-appropriate manner) might help, unless her uncle also used Bible study as part of the abuse scenario. She might be better off in Sunday school where a group setting with other children might feel safer. The teacher would need to be alerted to her issues and her possible questions. Lucy might ask whether or not God can be trusted to protect children, or even how the teacher feels about uncles who touch their nieces in the private areas (and nieces who allow it). Individual therapy with a Christian therapist, or at the very least one who could work with her on the theological issues that the abuse has raised, would be very important. All of this should be covered in prayer that the Holy Spirit would heal and comfort her. If she can tolerate going to church, participation in familiar rituals—the Eucharist, healing prayer or whatever may be common practice in her tradition—would be both comforting and spiritually helpful.

Amber is a seven-year-old girl who was sexually abused by her male babysitter for six months. It started with comparing body parts and progressed to his insisting that she touch his genitals with her hands and mouth. This felt dirty to her, and she told her parents about it after a Sunday school class on how God could wash you cleaner than clean when you felt dirty because of your sins. She feels proud that she told about her sitter touching her and believes God is proud of her for

talking about it. Her parents are devastated, blaming themselves for not picking
up on the fact that something was going on. They have pulled back from their
church out of shame because of what happened.

Amber's situation is similar to Lucy's, but the child and family have very different reactions from Lucy's family, and therefore different interventions are needed. Amber sees God as her ally—the one who could help her to feel clean again when she felt dirty and the one who is proud of her for doing the right thing even though it was hard when she told her parents about what happened with the sitter. She needs to be in church and Sunday school where this awareness of God as a resource and rock to be leaned on can be encouraged. Especially if there is to be child protective services involvement or a court proceeding, her ability to lean on and trust in God should be nurtured. There does not appear to be an underlying depression, and the psychiatric consultation and medication route does not seem needed for her. A major concern here is her parents, who seem to need help to come to some of the same understanding of God and his redeeming and forgiving love that their child has already reached. The local congregation needs to reach out to them so that they feel less judged. Amber does not appear to need group therapy, addressing the common issues related to child sexual abuse, but might profit from individual therapy to help her look at the changes in her family that followed upon her revealing her history of sexual abuse and how she and others in the family feel about what is happening now.

Different situations require different responses, and God is gracious enough to have provided a variety of healing approaches so that all might be touched by his Holy Sprit through direct experience of his healing presence, through his grace working through his people gathered in the church, or through others who work for healing even though the name of Jesus may not be mentioned. Even with God at work seeking to bring about healing, parents and others may worry about the long-term impact. Chapter eight examines what is known about the impact of childhood sexual abuse on development and later life and considers what can be done to lessen the impact these traumatic events have on a child's future.

8

What Does This Mean Long Term?

The Continuing Impact of the Abuse

"What I worry about, Rev. Williams, is where this leaves Mary long term. I mean, will she grow up to be a healthy, happy woman after all she went through with her Uncle Larry?"

"That's really hard to predict, Tom. A lot depends on her—how vulnerable she was to being damaged by the experience in the first place, how well she does with therapy and the other interventions that have been made available to her, and what happens in her life from here on."

"I understand that. There is no way to predict the future, and I guess I don't really expect that. But it seems like there should be some predictable danger zones and some sensible things we could do to reduce the chances of lasting damage."

"There are some typical issues, and some things that her mother and you can do to make it more likely that she will do well. Let me tell you about some of them."

One of the most typical worries for parents of children who have been sexually abused, once the shock of finding out and the whirlwind of dealing with the immediate concerns are over, is what the long-term effects will be.

The best answers the field of psychology has to offer today are somewhere between "we can't really predict for any specific case" and "there are certain problems that frequently arise and some interventions that can likely make these problems less severe." Both are true to some extent. Continued research and clinical observation have shed some light on what are frequent responses and give some clues as to what can be done to reduce the likelihood of damage.

There are two ways to attack the problem of understanding the long-term effects of child sexual abuse. The first and easiest way is to talk to people who were abused as children and seek to understand their common problems that can be traced back to their childhood trauma. The second is to start with a group of sexually abused children and follow their lives until they are adults to see what common problems develop and to determine what can be done to minimize such problems or reduce the likelihood that they will develop. Each approach has its strengths and weaknesses.

The ease of the first approach is coupled with the fact that the accuracy of the results is suspect. Which sexually abused children grow up to remember the abuse well enough to even categorize themselves as abuse survivors as adults? Or which remember but are too embarrassed or ashamed to admit to having been abused and so never even participate in whatever efforts have been made to gather data? How is the impact of other experiences—physical abuse or domestic violence, drug or alcohol involvement, unhealthy family life or other life events—accounted for and factored in to an understanding of what adult symptomatology was caused by the abuse and what was caused by other events in a person's life? These and other concerns can make it hard to know how to interpret whatever information is gleaned from this type of data collecting. Still, it can be important to look at the patterns that emerge even if they must be taken with a grain of salt due to intervening variables and possible bias of those reporting.

The second approach is problematic as well. Longitudinal studies are only beginning to yield their data. It is hard to follow any group for a long time—people move away or tire of participating in the study. The whole field of study of child sexual abuse is relatively young, and longitudinal studies by their very nature take a lot of time. Even with a willing subject pool it can be hard to conceptualize questions into a measurable format and assemble data into a meaningful form. Often by the time a question is narrowed down to the point where it can be assessed with the precision necessary for scientific study, the results may be too specific to generalize easily to the questions that parents and those who know and love the sexually abused child are asking.

Listening to Adults

We have learned from listening to adult survivors that relationships are often very hard for those who have been abused as children. These individuals, as they grow up, may veer off in one of two directions, either becoming emotionally withdrawn and having problems with intimacy, or having no boundaries and becoming emotionally and physically "overavailable." Adult survivors of child sexual abuse often find solace in physical closeness that disappoints even as it stimulates, since it touches only the body and not the heart.

For those who carry the pain of the abuse with them and bear the emotional aftermath that leads to isolation and loneliness, drug and alcohol involvement may appear a useful solution. Many adult survivors dull the pain with substance abuse, often finding that they can enter into relationships only when under the influence of a substance that makes intimacy less scary and more possible for them. Others drink or use drugs to escape problems with their family of origin or current family relationships.

Low self-esteem can be a long-term issue for adult survivors of child sexual abuse. Many feel they are to blame for the abusive events that happened, even though decades may have elapsed. For others, a sense of being different or not eligible for the good things that life might have in store continues, even though the reality basis for these feelings may have stopped decades earlier. A tragic cycle can be set up where the isolation and lack of social and vocational success that grew out of low self-esteem can further diminish a person's sense of competency and personal power. This in turn may lead to an ongoing lack of successes in relational and vocational spheres, which then reinforces the sense of failure and worthlessness. It can take courage and the help of determined friends, fellow believers and professional counselors to break out of this cycle.

Long-term depression can be a related problem. Adults who were abused as children may feel that since nothing good is going to come their way—or because they will end up wrecking anything good that *does* come—there is no use in trying to make things any different. Such irrational ideas are often amenable to a cognitive-behavioral therapy approach. Suicidal thoughts and even suicide attempts can also grow out of the unresolved issues of child sexual abuse.

Difficulty with families is another long-term consequence of child sexual abuse. At times this is because a member of the nuclear family was the abuser. At other times it grows out of the victim's belief that the family was not protective enough in allowing the abuse to occur in the first place or not supportive enough in dealing with the aftermath once the truth was known. It can be very difficult for child sexual abuse victims, as they grow up, to overcome the childhood-based fears and perceptions of family members and situations, so as to be able to relate well with these family members on an adult level. When they do, it frequently turns out that things have changed since their childhood, or at least some of their difficulties may be based on a child's understanding of situations that turn out to be very different when seen with adult eyes. For others the destructive patterns in their families of origin continue and can be seen more readily as everyone in the family gets older. There may be no other choice than to cut back on contact with a family that continues to be poisonous. In the worst-case scenario an adult abuse survivor finds that his or her family of origin continues to be a destructive, unsafe and crazy-making place for him or her. In this situation the survivor may need to cut himself or herself off entirely from the whole cast of characters, commending them in prayer to God, and trusting that God, who loves them far more than even the most devoted child can, will send others to reach them with his love, and through his Holy Spirit will call them to himself by grace. Healing and reconciliation may be found in Christ, but it often takes time and the willingness to face difficult and painful truths. Not everyone is willing or able to walk this road.

Issues with God are also common. For some abused children there is an immediate loss of faith in a God who could allow abuse to occur. This loss of faith may be sudden and long-lasting. Others find that they question their belief in God as they mature and reflect back on the abusive experiences. They may gradually come to believe in a God who is not all-powerful or all-loving as they seek to make sense out of how the God whom they thought they knew could have allowed such a thing to happen.

For people who were abused sexually at a young age, normal developmental and social maturation will require a rethinking of the abusive experience and may lead to new or recurring symptoms. Developmentally normal shifts in the ways children conceptualize and understand their world may require new analyses of the abusive experience as they enter the new stages of concrete operations (around age six or seven), formal operations (around ten) and abstract thinking (around the early teens). A child who is moving away from the self-centered thinking of the preschool period may suddenly ask, "Hey, didn't Uncle Tommy ever stop to think how bad *I* was going to feel after what he did to me?" as he or she is increasingly able to take another's point of view in relationships. Similarly, a teen moving into the abstract operations stage may ask big questions (often of moral or philosophical nature) that didn't occur at earlier stages of thinking: "If God is loving and forgives Uncle Tommy for touching me, since Uncle Tommy is a Christian and asked for forgiveness, then where is the justice for me and what I went through?" This type of change and questioning is normal and part of the development of every child. A child who was abused has that additional piece of history to work through. For some, the details of the abuse fade into the past and are not actively reconsidered at each stage of development. This is another normal pattern and is not necessarily indicative of problems.

Some children, as they mature, will rework the abusive experience as they move into different relational patterns with adults and peers. A child who experienced the abuse as a violation of trust and sees adults with a wary eye will have different feelings toward a coach, drama club director or favorite youth leader than one who has not had this experience. He or she may be more cynical of the motivation of the adult who is working with children, or may have more difficulty trusting the positive feelings that a good experience with a skilled, youth-oriented adult engenders. There is also the opportunity for a corrective emotional experience when the adult proves to be trustworthy, kind and honest, if the child can tolerate the anxiety of the relationship long enough to get this benefit. As peer relationships change, many children will have to revisit their abusive experience as they begin to become emotionally intimate with others and again at the time of initial, consensual peer-sexual relationships. Emotional and sexual intimacy may frighten them and cause them to pull back from relationships when the feelings and actions are too similar to the abusive experience. Conversely, having already had an adult sexual relationship thrust upon them before they could experience it with an adult body, adult feelings and an adult intellectual understanding of what was happening, some child abuse survivors find as they grow that they slide too easily past landmarks, boundaries and decision points that many of their peers would pause at. They may wrongly be labeled promiscuous or rejected as immoral, while they need understanding and help in developing another way of responding to their abusive experiences. Both possible reactions need to be monitored and processed with an understanding adult who is aware of the child's abuse history and the patterns often found in the development of children who have experienced sexual abuse.

Learning from the Children

Longitudinal studies of abused children yield both expected and unexpected results. Many of the issues already discussed turn up as potent results of child sexual abuse in the lives of children. Some children seem not to have been greatly impacted at all, while others have a much harder time, developing severe psychosocial problems such as substance abuse, sexual dysfunction, major depression, suicidal behavior and posttraumatic stress disorder. Research has focused on trying to find out what makes the difference—that is, what are the variables that seem to account for why some children do better than others? While we may never reach a 100 percent understanding of why a particular child copes better than his or her peers, due in part to the tremendous variation in individual responses to abuse, it is helpful to look at the research findings.

Many studies have looked at factors that might impact the effects of child sexual abuse, such as the type and duration of the abuse, the identity of the abuser, the recency of the abuse or the use of force. Results are inconsistent and inconclusive about how these factors impact a child's response and ability to cope later in life. What does appear to make a major difference is parental support and the parents' response to the child's disclosure. Children who receive emotional support from a nonoffending adult are likely to be less symptomatic. Conversely, negative reactions from a child's mother tend to predict more severe reactions.

The implications of these findings are hopeful. The factors over which the child and those seeking to help the child have no control, such as the frequency and severity of the abuse or the identity of the abuser, may be less important than some factors that *can* be controlled, such as the support of a nonabusive adult or maternal empathy and care. These positive factors can make a tremendous difference in a child's life.

What Can Be Done

Both the research done with the children and the retrospective studies of adult survivors of child sexual abuse suggest that there is hope. Since parental reaction and support may be the single most important predictor of a child's successful coping with abuse, families should be given encouragement and support so that they can be emotionally present for their children. Similarly, nonoffending adults—Sunday school teachers, youth leaders and other adults in the church—can be of crucial importance in the healing of children and adolescents; they can and should be trained to shoulder this responsibility. When children have the opportunity to talk with caring, well-trained adults about the sexual-abuse incidents and the feelings that they caused, they have a better chance of becoming symptom free.

The issue of training for those who minister in churches and para-church ministries—not only for interventions made after the fact, such as those highlighted in this chapter, but before abuse is known to have occurred, during disclosure and immediately afterward while the family is still in shock—is of crucial importance. Chapter nine addresses this subject and discusses how a church can become proactive in the area of child sexual abuse.

9

Could It Happen Here?

Proactive Preparation to Become an Abuse-Aware Church

> "Hey, Rev. Thompson, I saw that report about what happened over at First Church last weekend."
>
> "It was awful, wasn't it? A Sunday school teacher and a seven-year-old girl! The church should be the safest place, not the place where kids get hurt."
>
> "You know, my cousin Jimmy goes there. He says no one ever suspected the guy who did it. He was new to the church, but he'd been teaching Sunday school at his old church—at least that's what he said."
>
> "I'm glad we never had any problems like that."
>
> "Me too, but it got me thinking. Are we doing all that we could be doing to make sure we never have a problem like that? Could it happen here?"

This conversation, or one like it, happens all over the country each time another church makes the six o'clock news with a story of child abuse.

The question "Could it happen here?" must be answered yes. Whenever people gather together to accomplish any good purpose for God, they bring their brokenness and pain—and with it the potential of harming others, both unintentionally and by design. There is no way to guarantee total safety for children and to be absolutely certain that child sexual abuse will never occur in any given church. The question "Could it happen here?" can never be answered with a definite no. But each church and parachurch organization needs to face honestly another question: Are we doing all we can to make sure that our children are safe and that abuse is as unlikely as possible? This final chapter addresses the process of becoming an abuse-aware church, learning how to take steps to be proactive rather than waiting to react after trouble comes, and integrating protective abuse awareness into the fabric of the life of a healthy community.

There are several aspects to the process of building a community that is proactive concerning child sexual abuse without becoming overwhelmed by fear of it.

☐ *Awareness.* People must understand that abuse can and does happen even in the best of communities, even with the best volunteer and paid staff. Until the denial that says "it can't happen here" is broken, the risk factor for every child in the community is higher.

☐ *Education.* Every staff person, volunteer and member of the congregation must be informed concerning abuse-related issues and knowledgeable about safety and self-protection. Education increases awareness, and as the subject is brought out of the darkness and into the light, the safety issues related to this topic can and should be discussed as they apply to all aspects of the life of a ministry or community.

☐ *Planning.* Specific, concrete steps must be identified to decrease the likelihood of child sexual abuse and increase the safety of children, volunteers and staff.

☐ *Implementation.* The very best plans amount to nothing if they are not put into action. Even a poor plan, implemented in a way that increases safety of children by the smallest amount, is better than the most sophisticated plan that is never funded or carried out.

☐ *Assessment and feedback.* Those impacted by the plan, both children and adults, should be given the opportunity to give feedback as to how the procedures affect the ministry and life of the community, and changes should be made based upon this input.

☐ *Integration.* Finally, all of this needs to be lived out in the life of the community, without becoming so burdensome that the quality of the ministry suffers irreparable damage or people cut corners to avoid what is perceived as an onerous burden of abuse-related rules and regulations. The commitment to the prevention of, detection of and ministry to those impacted by child sexual abuse must be integrated into the mission and practices of the community. Each of these issues will be discussed in turn.

Awareness

Establishing an *awareness* of child sexual abuse can be difficult. People do not want to consider the possibility that this issue may come knocking at their own church doors. It may take a well-publicized event in a neighboring church or community to break through the self-protective veil that keeps us from seeing the reality that the children in our own Sunday school classrooms, youth groups and junior choirs are at risk. In addition to the difficulty of seeing the potential danger *to* their own children, many congregations have trouble believing that there exists a potential danger *from* their members as well. Child abusers may go to other churches, but kindly Mrs. Jones, who has been teaching Sunday school for twenty-five years, or that nice young couple, the Bridges, who moved in last year, could never be suspect. As an understanding grows that all children are at risk and any adult could be an abuser, the church will see the need to take steps to protect both the children and the adults involved in ministry to children.

An additional benefit of increased awareness is that, as the subject is mentioned in board meetings or the Sunday worship service or in Sunday school information sent home to parents, it becomes a topic that can safely be addressed in the context of the worshiping community. Families with a child who has been abused will feel more comfortable talking to a pastor or lay leader about their needs if the church demonstrates an understanding of the special problems that may exist in this area. Others who suspect that something is going on with their child will be more willing to turn to the church for support and assistance as the church demonstrates a willingness to face the issue.

Education

Once an awareness of the problem has begun to take hold of a congregation, people will be open to *education* concerning the scope of the issue, the ways it may impact the life of the congregation, what to do when it is suspected or confirmed in members of the body, and how to reduce the possibility of child sexual abuse occurring on church property or with church staff. This education should take place on all levels to be effective, beginning with the senior minister and staff members, extending to Sunday school teachers, youth group workers and other volunteers, and finally reaching all members. Pastoral staff should read up on the ways to identify and minister to child sexual abuse, attending seminars offered by professionals if these are available in their vicinity. Legal issues should be considered, such as the liability that the church incurs if a staff member or volunteer molests a child, or who has responsibility to make a report to the state child welfare agency when abuse becomes known. The church should contact insurance agents to find out what coverage exists and the limits of coverage in this area. Some insurance companies void their insurance unless specific policies and procedures are in place and followed in the screening, hiring and training of staff and volunteers. Church leadership should be aware of the requirements of their own insurance programs and make sure they are satisfied. And they should teach their leaders ways to minister to children and adults who are dealing with child sexual abuse in their families.

Education about child sexual abuse should be made a part of the ongoing teaching and training ministry of the church. Legal requirements for reporting and the internal policies and procedures developed by a church can be covered in the initial training of Sunday school teachers prior to the beginning of the church school year. Staff and volunteers should be screened routinely at the beginning of their work with the church, and the church's policies on abuse should be discussed with them before they are allowed to work with children and families. It may be possible to have a Child Abuse Sunday in which the needs of those who deal with this issue are highlighted and ways to minister effectively to them are discussed. Or it may work better in the life of a particular congregation to address the issue as it comes up in Sunday sermons. For example, a teaching on Jesus' blessing of the children in Matthew or Mark could include Jesus' warning that those who lead one of the little ones astray will meet with severe judgment. The sermon may be an open door for discussion of the topic without making that the sole focus of the Scripture lesson. Whatever the format for a particular church, an issue that statistics show is likely to impact as many as 30 percent of its people cannot be overlooked.

Planning

Awareness and education lead to *planning*. Policies and procedures need to be reviewed and rewritten to make certain that the area of child sexual abuse is adequately covered. This is especially important in the areas of staff and volunteer hiring, child abuse reporting responsibilities, pastoral care of potentially abusive staff and volunteers, and ministry to children and families when child sexual abuse is alleged. There are also important implications for the day-to-day activities of a church or parachurch ministry.

Staff and volunteers should be required to fill out a written application for their positions. Among other questions, they need to be asked directly, "Have you ever been accused of or convicted of child abuse?" A positive answer need not automatically disqualify an applicant but should lead to a thorough discussion of the circumstances of the accusation or conviction. If, for instance, the applicant tells of an accusation that came out of a desire for revenge or from an angry parent, this may be less serious than if he or she tells of a conviction by jury trial. A negative answer may not be true; abusers do lie to gain access to children or in an attempt to escape their past, but the fact that the question has been asked underlines the importance of the issue and reassures parents that the church takes seriously its responsibility to be protective of the children surrendered to its care. Another potential benefit of asking the question is that a predatory abuser looking to gain access to children may move on to another location when he or she finds that it is not easy to get to the children at a particular church. You might also ask questions such as "Why do you want to be a youth group leader [Sunday school teacher, nursery care provider]?" "What do you like to do in your spare time?" or "Name three adults who know you well who could recommend you for this position." Such questions may help to screen out the person who overly identifies with children, has little adult contact in his or her life, and seeks to meet his or her own emotional needs through working with children. These people are more likely to be abusers. (In addition to screening out potential problems related to child sexual abuse, written job applications can be of use in assessing drug and alcohol problems, a history of violence or whatever other aspect of human behavior the church feels is important to screen out when considering a volunteer or staff appointment.)

It is also a good idea to routinely ask those who will have access to children and vulnerable populations in ministry to agree to give permission for their records to be checked with the state child abuse registry or the registry of convicted child sexual abusers (if that is publicly available in your area). This permission can be incorporated into a release form included in the job application. It may be added to areas such as a driving record history (to check for driving under the influence convictions for those who would be transporting others in the course of their ministry at the church) or history of conviction of a felony, which may already be a part of a church's hiring process.

At the time of job application or hire, the staff member or volunteer should also be made aware of any church policy and procedures regarding the reporting of abuse and the management of staff or volunteers accused of abuse by those to whom they minister. Applicants should sign off on a statement that they have received these policies and had them explained to them. (Additional training may be required in the course of moving into actively exercising a ministry; again, written records should be kept of all those trained or exempted from training.)

Policies and procedures regarding the reporting of suspected sexual abuse should be clear and explained to all staff. Legal guidance should be obtained in the writing of the policies to make certain that they meet the requirements of state laws. Generally, clergy are mandated reporters of suspected child abuse. This means that they must notify state child protective services orally and in writing within a specified period of time when they *suspect* child abuse. Note that they do not need to be certain that abuse is occurring and are not required by the law to undertake an investigation. Rather, they are mandated to notify those who are trained to do such an investigation whenever they suspect that a child may be being abused. This can be very difficult to do, especially if the suspected abuser is a member of the congregation and an acquaintance or friend. Yet the law is clear on what is required of mandated reporters. Clarity in policy and procedures will make it easier for clergy to follow through with their responsibility since the steps are clearly enumerated. If the clergy can point to specific policies and procedures approved by the church officers and governing boards, it will be easier for them to share the blame when those who are offended by their making the report complain to the church leaders. Clearly spelled out expectations that clergy will comply with state reporting laws will also help to hold clergy accountable for following through with this often difficult and distasteful task.

Who in addition to the clergy will be expected to make child abuse reports? Some churches have taken the position that *all* volunteers and staff are considered mandated reporters for the purposes of compliance with state child abuse reporting laws. Others designate a person who is a mandated reporter (typically a clergy person or a licensed counselor if there is one on the church staff) to be the key person to whom all suspicions of child abuse are reported. That person then makes all abuse reports for the church. Of course, the person to whom the information that led to a suspicion of child abuse was originally made known can make a report, even if the designated reporter decides not to do so, and some states have provisions in their laws specifically addressing this situation to make sure that there are no repercussions within a place of employment for a person who decides to do so.

Written policies and procedures should also specify what actions will be taken if staff members or volunteers are accused of child sexual abuse either within the context of their ministry or elsewhere in their lives. The best time to decide issues of paid versus unpaid leave, partial duties that limit access to children, or requirements for counseling is before the need

arises. The two extremes between which a balance must be struck are the
need to protect children from a potentially abusive interaction and the
need to maintain toward an accused staff person a stance that is in keeping
with the "innocent until proven guilty" basis of our law. Legal advice may
need to be sought to ensure compliance with state law as this policy is
crafted. If it is not thought through ahead of time, issues of personality and
emotional assessments of both the accused and the accuser enter into the
picture and confuse the thinking of everyone involved.

The issue of whether allegations of abuse outside the workplace (for
example, by a spouse who, in the midst of a tempestuous divorce proceeding, claims that a child was abused) should impact an individual's work
responsibilities must also be carefully considered. It is not necessarily the
case that a person accused of abusing a child in an intimate relationship
would also be at risk for doing so in a ministry situation. Yet it represents a
risk to both the children receiving services and the integrity of the ministry
to let an accused molester continue to have access to children in a ministry
situation with no constraints placed upon their activities. This matter
should also be carefully thought through with policies in place before the
situation arises.

In addition to planning how to handle the reporting of abuse, should
the suspicion of abuse arise, planning teams should consider how to minister to families in the congregation who are living in an abusive situation or
dealing with the aftermath of abuse having been reported. Earlier chapters
discussed some of the issues common to these situations. It is wise for a
ministry to have in place a plan for helping families. On the most practical
level, who will assist with meeting the day-to-day needs of families responding to an abusive episode in their lives, and how will their needs be com-
municated to those designated to help? It is seldom necessary to tell the
reason that a family needs help to all those involved in providing the help,
but some sort of explanation should be prepared with the assistance of the
family so that rumors and gossip are kept to a minimum. The long-term
needs of a family caught in the system and dealing with the aftermath of an
abusive episode may exhaust those in the church who typically respond to
needs. Their needs must be monitored and attended to as well.

In addition to the extraordinary circumstances considered so far, care must be taken to reexamine the daily operations of the church with child sexual abuse issues in mind. For example, for maximum safety *no adult should ever be alone in private with a child or group of children.* This is for the protection of both the adult and the children. If not left alone, a potential abuser has less opportunity to have access to a child. If no adult is alone with a child or group of children, there can be no allegations of child sexual abuse by a child without an adult witness also having been present at the time in question. This can be a difficult commitment to make and live out—it means that every Sunday school class, youth group, or nursery/daycare situation must have two people at all times: no one can step out to go to the bathroom, take the collection to the office or make more copies of the class material. Yet, despite the difficulty, the importance of making this commitment and keeping to it cannot be overemphasized. This should also be extended to the role of adults driving children to or from church activities, the role of choir directors or church play coordinators working with soloists or lead actors, and all adults working with children no matter how well-intentioned the adult or how comfortable the child. In situations where this is impossible, be sure there are windows in doors to rooms where children's ministry occurs, and enforce a policy of drop-by visits by clergy, lay leadership and parents while ministry is going on.

Other implications of being child sexual abuse proactive that might change the way things are done are simple precautions, such as not letting anyone be in a ministry situation with children until they have been in the church at least one year and are known to the ministers and church leadership. If they come to the church from another ministry situation, they should be asked to put in writing their permission for the current leadership to talk to those in charge of their ministry in their former location. While it is possible that the information given might not be true, by asking the questions, it is possible that problematic situations might be avoided.

Doors should all have windows in them. No child should be taken to the bathroom by one adult alone. Parents should be called in to assist a child who needs toileting help. Every aspect of ministry should be reconsidered in the light of abuse issues.

Implementation

The next step is putting into practice the plans, policies and procedures. The best ideas are worthless if *implementation* does not follow. For most churches the hardest part of building a safer community is the human factor. Staff and volunteers may be reticent to follow through with aspects of the procedures that they see as cumbersome, inefficient or different from the ways things have always been done. Good supervision and persuasive leadership can help people to see the need for these common-sense approaches. The long-term risk to children, staff and volunteers, and indirectly to the church through bad publicity and lawsuits, outweighs the short-term inconvenience of doing things the right way to protect children. While the precautions mentioned above may seem unnecessary, and may in fact be unnecessary more times than not, it is precisely because one cannot predict in advance which times they will be needed that they must be observed at all times.

Other obstacles to intervention can include obtaining the necessary training or finding the necessary material for parents, staff and children. Searching the Internet may be a good way to find opportunities for training that are nearby. Contacting denominational or church association resources may also yield helpful connections.

Assessment and Feedback

In some ways the connecting loop that brings everything back to the first step of awareness is *assessment and feedback*. As church members' awareness of abuse issues grows and the church is successful in becoming a community where child sexual abuse is a permissible subject to talk about, leadership will begin to hear from the members what they like and don't like about the way the subject has been handled. What works and what doesn't work will become clearer. As this awareness increases, more *education* and *planning* will lead to changes to make church systems even better. It is important to set times and dates for assessment and feedback (or else it will never happen) and to include input from all parts of the church body.

Integration

Finally, the goal of *integration* may be fulfilled. Awareness of the danger of child sexual abuse and the steps needed to increase safety and assist children and families are *integrated* into the life of the church, so that no one can remember a time when these matters were not talked about. No one thinks twice anymore about following the child sexual abuse prevention precautions, which have become a natural part of doing things. Reaching this goal may take some time, but when a church or ministry gets to that point, children will be safer from child sexual abuse, families will be helped if it should occur, and volunteers and staff will be equipped to handle the situation if and when it arises.

If this were a work of fiction, we might end with the words "and they all lived happily ever after." That is too simple an ending for a book such as this, which deals with the painful and complex events of people's real lives. Yet I hope that the information and suggestions given here will help many people, as they deal with the trauma of child sexual abuse, to see a future beyond their immediate pain. Healing does come. No matter how difficult the circumstances, there is hope.

CPSIA information can be obtained
at www.ICGtesting.com
Printed in the USA
LVHW03s2302190618
581338LV00002B/230/P

9 780830 822461